THE L(

THE LONG SEARCH

Terry Jarvis
with Lin Ball

Hope it Touch'd the Spot!

T Jarvis

The names in this book have been changed out of consideration for those who appear.

Line drawings by Pam Holloway.

Copyright © Terry Jarvis tjarvis770000@yahoo.co.uk

ISBN 978-1-4710-2907-3

FOREWORD

I'm a wood carver with a special love for working with driftwood. Right now I'm planning to create an original lamp from a large and beautiful piece that is deeply grooved and lined from the effects of the ocean. I call it 'the castle in the sky' because that's what I see in its shape. I want to mount it on a curved white pebble base and light the 'walls' and 'windows' and 'turrets' from below.

My piece of driftwood has been shaped so creatively by the action of the waves – just as my life has been shaped by events, circumstances, difficulties and trials. The rough and smooth parts of my character have been moulded by the days that have gone before. I have been tested and tried as a person. As you will read, by the age of 22 I had travelled much of the world, largely in pursuit of making money through drug smuggling. Although at one time I had a great deal of money, I discovered I was empty inside.

Since I was a young kid I believed there was a God. But after my mum died of a brain tumour and I found myself in the care system I gave up praying. Despite the instability of my teenage years, deep down I always felt a connection with God. However, my interest in spirituality took me on my travels into many religions and the occult. It was only when I literally got to the end of myself that I cried out to God in desperation. He heard me and I began a whole new life.

THE LONG SEARCH tells the story of that journey and my prayer is that it will be meaningful to all those who read it.

Where am I today? Still on a journey, many years later... still learning and with more to discover about God.

Since those early days of finding new life in Christ and trying to make sense of it all, God has been good and gracious to me. I have so much to thank him for, not least my loving and faithful wife and companion Sue. We have four wonderful grown children who I love to spend time with; and seven grandchildren who bring me great joy.

Soon after the writing of THE LONG SEARCH, Sue and I felt God leading us to live in Cumbria and we've been there ever since. The story of how we followed that calling and how God met our needs for accommodation and employment is another book in itself. I believe God gave me a vision for the town where we live – a vision which has only partly been fulfilled and which has been a source of both joy and sorrow to me as I have wrestled with it over the years. Ephesians 2:10 says '...we are God's workmanship, created in Christ Jesus to do good works, which God prepared in advance for us to do.' I want to spend my life discovering those good works God has prepared for me, and doing my best to carry them out.

Becoming a craftsman has been very fulfilling. To woodcarving I have added skills in antique and furniture restoration, upholstery, cane work, sculpture and painting. I have learned that it's deeply satisfying to be working at what you enjoy rather than enduring the grind of employment just for the sake of a wage to pay the bills. I believe this is the way God wants us to live. I try to share that truth with others and have developed an assessment course to help people identify their true career gifting from what's really in their hearts. When you enjoy your daily work, self-motivation is absolutely no problem and neither is sticking at it. Working with wood in particular gives me deep fulfilment and I want others to discover their talents – whatever they may be – and have the same experience. Realising your talents is not just limited to arts and crafts; some people discover creative ability in management or sales, in teaching, in outdoor activities, in care work.

I have a workshop alongside a railway station. My door is always open and every new customer becomes a friend as we spend time together. I love nothing better than to invite in a troubled young person to work shoulder to shoulder with me on some craft project, building up an atmosphere of trust in which I can share some of my own experiences and talk about the Jesus who rescued me. All the time I meet young people who are going through some of the things I describe in THE LONG SEARCH. It's humbling. But often I spend hours working alone in my workshop – and then I take pleasure in reflecting on God's powerful Word, the Bible. I take time to think about my aim to acknowledge Him in all I do; and about my longing to give more importance to the spiritual than the material.

Over the years I've had many opportunities to share God's Word with others – specifically during six years as pastor of a small church, and also through openings to go into the local prison and schools to share my life story. I've also had the amazing experience of spending three weeks in war-torn Burundi in Africa, sharing the gospel. The poverty and openness of the people deeply impacted me.

So, to return to that piece of driftwood... God is still developing my character. He longs for each of us to become more like Jesus. I am intrigued by how God is changing me, as I do my best to be open to Him and see Him in everything. I am encouraged by many characters in the Bible – Paul, Joseph and Job, for example – whose lives were deeply shaped by very difficult circumstances. I know that in my life God has been in it all – both the good and the tough times.

Terry Jarvis, 2011
tjarvis770000@yahoo.co.uk

INTRODUCTION

A busy Saturday in Kingston, London. An unlikely place for such a drama, but even before I saw him on the bridge a sense of the unusual was with me.

He was a big lad with short fair hair. With one arm he gripped the parapet of the bridge, the other was wildly waving his jacket. My eyes fixed on the terror on his face as I dashed through the traffic. Cars slowed, people paused, shading their eyes and frowning. But not going to him. Anger about their lack of caring swept over me and pushed me towards him. I was nearly there, seeing now his blue short-sleeved shirt, his wide eyes, the spectacles clutched in his hand together with his jacket, flapping, held out over the water. I saw the white knuckles on the bridge.

'Don't, please don't!' I grabbed fiercely at him and clutched the top of his arm.

'Don't jump!'

He pulled away and was gone. Over the edge and down. I heard the sound of hurrying feet and felt behind me the pressing wall of the crowd. They peered into the water, curious but distant. And yet again the anger welled up inside me.

I pulled off my shoes. I was aware of Sue, shocked and quiet at my side. Pulling my money from my jeans pocket I pressed it into her hand. I felt stiff and clumsy as I clambered onto the ledge. And before I could get myself ready for a dive – I tripped.

Thirty feet down, I hit the water hard and sank into a terrifying grey-green world, cold and dark. After what seemed an age as long as a nightmare I rose up again into the brightness, my lungs bursting. I caught sight of the blue shirt just a few yards away and reached out towards it. As I grabbed him he struggled, twisting round and pressing me down under the water. I fought my way up, coughing and gasping. I yelled now. 'Help, someone! Help!' Weakness was creeping through my body with cold fingers.

Suddenly I saw the boat. A grey-haired man in a summer shirt and dark trousers was at the steering wheel. Behind him a thin suntanned woman lay back in a seat. I yelled again. The man glanced sideways at me and then his lips tightened and he turned away from me, gripping the wheel.

'Wait... stop! No! Help!' The words struggled from me as I thrashed about in the water. I shouted several times, but he continued to ignore me.

And, amazingly, that was when his engine cut out. I heard it splutter as he tried to restart it, then all I could hear was the slap slapping of the waves against the boat as it turned slowly, drifting with the current. Drifting towards me! Now the woman stood, nervously glancing all around. She picked up a short piece of fraying orange string hanging from the bows and threw it towards me. I ignored it and struck out with the last of my strength towards the boat, grabbing the rough edge and hauling myself exhausted over the side.

Then there was the canoe that drew alongside, seeming to appear from nowhere. It was being paddled by a silent young man whose calm, almost serene, face was framed with long blond hair. The shaking wet body of the boy who had jumped off the bridge was clinging to the front of the canoe. I leaned over and pulled him into the boat.

The canoe went softly on its way and I held the limp body in my arms and let him cry.

The rest of the incident passed in a clamour of activity, noise and excitement. The police arrived and asked lots of questions. Someone in the boatyard gave me some dry clothes. Then I was in the back of the ambulance. Vic – that was the boy's name – lay white and unseeing under a grey blanket. The ambulance attendant droned on and on.

'Now look at all the trouble you've gone and caused everyone… it just don't make sense. A young man too, whole of your life in front of you, why… there's just no reason. . .' There was a hard edge to his voice I hated.

I leaned over the blanket, trying to manage a smile, though my throat was sore and my eyes felt strange and swollen.

'Vic, you're going to be all right, don't worry now. I know how you feel. I know how it hurts. Believe me, I do. . . You see, I've been there myself. Six or seven times I've tried to take my own life. With drugs mostly. Overdose. But that's all in the past. I found a new life, when I discovered that Jesus Christ is a real person. Finding out about Jesus has changed my life completely. '

Vic looked at me. He said nothing – but his eyes seemed to shout for help.

The ambulance man rubbed his hands together nervously. He coughed and stared at his feet.

'Well, now, this ain't somethin' I'd tell just anyone,' he began softly. His voice was quite different now, low and confidential.

'It's about the wife. She says she can't take no more. She says she's havin' a sort of breakdown. Nerves it is. She talks about doin' away with herself. I just don't know what to do.'

The sadness was there again, welling up from deep inside me. I desperately wanted to help them both and felt so weak.

'O Lord, give me the words to say! Please give me the right words to say to them,' I prayed.

CHAPTER 1

The story of the attempted suicide and my attempted rescue was in all the local papers. I've still got all the cuttings somewhere. There was even a reception in the mayor's parlour and a certificate from the Royal Humane Society, all of which seemed, then as now, a bit unnecessary. Still, it did give me a good chance to tell people about my own story, which by any standards is a bit out of the ordinary to say the least. And I felt that perhaps the time had come to do that. The reporters were quite interested, even if they did find a lot of it hard to grasp! Still, when God's involved in anything you must expect that some things just can't be completely explained by human logic. Like the engine on that boat cutting out when it did. Or the canoe, which mysteriously appeared from nowhere and couldn't be traced afterwards. Just coincidences? Well, I'll leave you to judge that.

The local police in Kingston were quite interested in the story, too. The rescue incident didn't quite fit in with what they had on file about Terry Jarvis!

Looking back, the best way that I can come to terms with it all myself is to think of it as a search. And that makes sense of everything.

Aren't most of us searching, although it may be unconsciously? True, there are different goals, different gods. Some people are looking for material gain, power, influence over others. Their achievement is measured in physical terms, in bricks and mortar, in hard cash, in votes counted. Others search the intangible. They're looking for peace, personally or universally. They're looking for self understanding. Or simply happiness. Or that wonderful experience we call love. If that's the kind of search you're on, then the satisfaction is not always easy to measure. Probably only you yourself know how far along the road you've travelled. And who can say how much further there is to go?

My own search began pretty early in life. My childhood was much like that of hundreds of kids living in London in the 1950s. There were six of us in the family. Gary was the oldest, then me, followed by Linda, Philip, Sue, Sharon.

Dad had been a boxer in the Royal Navy many years before and then ran his own fishmongery business. He worked long hours – we didn't see much of him at all. Mum was loving and homely, very patient and thoughtful towards each one of us. I always pictured her in the kitchen, bent over the table making fish cakes. She was a good cook and always knew how to make the best out of what she had. But when I was quite young she was taken seriously ill. Dad just couldn't just cope with us and the business, so we were all split up among a succession of children's homes.

One home I was in remains a particularly vivid memory. Hook Heath Farm it was called, a huge house just outside Woking. The path to it wound up a hill, over a stream, over a railway bridge through a dense wood. Then past the golf course and the pond and there it was at the end of a gravel driveway. To the left was the 'Dell', a marvellous, swampy jungle of thickets that was simply great for kids to play in.

'You don't have to call us Mum and Dad...' said Mrs Hayes. But what she meant was, 'Everyone else does, you'd better do the same if you know what's good for you!' She was a stocky little woman with dark curled hair, a sharp tongue and a short temper. And she ran Hook Heath Farm in the time-honoured regimental way.

The discipline came hard to me. I was ten and it was my first time away from home. I was worried about Mum, missed my brothers and sisters, and Dad wasn't able to visit very much. Right from the start I just didn't seem to get it right – one scrape led to another.

One day early on, it was a little toy drill that got me into trouble. The set routine for each afternoon after school was that as soon as we got in we had to go to the cloakroom, clean our shoes, put them into numbered boxes and wait in the playroom for tea. But the rule was – no toys out before the meal. That afternoon was the last day of term and I was so excited I just had to break that rule. I got out my little toy drill and got stuck into one of my favourite games – whittling away at a small lump of chalk. But I got caught! And the punishment ordered by Mrs Hayes was that every day for a whole week – the first week of the summer holiday – I had to stand in solitary confinement on the spot facing the wall, with just the shortest breaks possible for meals.

I don't remember what I thought about during those long lonely hours, but I don't think repentance was uppermost in my mind! I wasn't a good boy. I'd been the sort of child who was always getting into trouble at home and had no reason to change here. Frequent canings had no beneficial effect, either. The truth is that during my time at the children's home I became a proficient petty thief. Stealing from the village shops was a speciality that gave me a position among the rest of the boys I couldn't earn any other way. I even broke into the church on the common and stole from the collection box on the wall. I went to visit that same church recently, to walk around it and remember, to feel sorrow for the past and joy for the present. But regret wasn't an experience I'd come across in those far-off days.

No, I was a troublemaker all right. And I led others into trouble, too. We used to get up to some pretty daring pranks: having climbing races up and down the massive old beech trees in the grounds, lashing together planks and bits of old bikes to make chariots, stealing sausages and cooking them out in the open. I learned the arts of survival, self-preservation and deception. And I learned them well.

Dad says my own picture of myself was always as the black sheep of the family and perhaps it was a role I decided to make for myself. Whatever the truth of it, I always felt out of place in that children's home.

Mum's blackouts got more serious, and then she died of a brain tumour. The day Dad told us all is another one of those memories that never fade. He collected us all in the dining room at Hook Heath Farm. My brother Philip had been moved to Hook Heath by this time, and the others had been brought over from the home they were staying in at Guildford. I sat and stared at the flames licking round the coal in the open grate.

'Be brave,' Dad said to me: 'Stick your chest out like a man.' He was always telling me to be brave, brave as a boxer. But he didn't look too brave himself that day as he broke the news to all of us.

That night I heard Philip crying from the next dormitory. I slipped out of bed and went to put my arms round him. But, after just a few minutes, Mrs Hayes appeared like some dreadful ghost in the doorway, clutching her trailing dressing gown at her neck.

'Get back into bed this instant,' she barked.

'But Philip's crying,' I said, weakly.

'I don't care about that – get back to your own bed now or else!'

That night was the last night I said my childish prayers. There didn't seem a lot of point any more, and even the comfort of those familiar phrases I'd learnt at Sunday School seemed to have gone, like nursery rhymes you grow out of.

I ran away from the home several times but got caught and taken back. After I'd been there about a year some of us older kids got a petition together and sent it to the County Council complaining about the punishments. We weren't hopeful of getting anything changed, but soon afterwards a real battleaxe of a woman in a tweed suit and funny hat arrived and asked us all a lot of questions. A few months later Mrs Hayes was moved to a smaller home and some new houseparents arrived – but I was moved on anyway at about that time.

From Hook Heath I went to Pinehurst, a home near Farnham in Surrey, and continued to practise the art of survival for the next few years. At the age of fifteen

I got my first real opportunity to escape the system. I joined the Army. Not only did I join but I enjoyed the life and did well. After some training as a drummer I was sent to Germany on a training course – two weeks' orienteering. But when I got back to camp in Canterbury I had a bit of a shock that was to put a stop to this short-lived success. Clare, the girl I'd been going out with, said she was pregnant. With no one to advise me I did what I thought I should do. I resorted to the classic way of getting myself kicked out of the Army. By committing a total of thirty charges I got myself dismissed!

As it turned out I needn't have bothered.

'Sorry, Terry, anyone can make a mistake...'

Clare wasn't pregnant after all! We didn't stay together much longer, as I decided to sign on as a cabin boy in the Merchant Navy. This turned out to be another far from romantic episode in my early life. The assorted crew was either violent, homosexual or messing about with drugs, and I lived in continual fear of all of them.

Scared and miserable, I spent hours alone at night perched on a coil of rope on the deck, staring at the sea and sky and wondering what life was really all about. Deep down, I hoped there was something far more wonderful than anything I had experienced so far. One night when we docked at Cardiff on a return trip from France, I told the captain I was leaving. I was so desperate to get away I would have pulled a knife on him if he'd tried to stop me.

Perhaps it's small surprise that back in London I adopted a way of life characterised by petty crime and gang fights. This was the era of the Mods and Rockers of the 1960s and I wanted to be where the action was. Did I say 'action'? Well, in fact I spent most of the next three years decidedly out of the action – behind locked doors! I served a string of sentences for thieving, breaking and entering, and burglary.

The first time I was sentenced to a stay in Ashford Remand Centre I behaved like a typical seventeen-year-old offender, trying to act and talk as if I didn't care two hoots for anyone in authority.

I was shivering as the door slammed shut on the blue coach with cubicles they used to take us from the courts to the remand centre – the 'meat wagon' as we called it! I put on the usual insolent act for the man in white jacket and Hitler-peaked cap with the job of writing down all my particulars and in the end he left me alone in the room for four hours – 'to cool off', he said. Then a prison officer arrived and ordered me to strip off so that he could subject me to the humiliating procedure of searching me for drugs. After the regulation bath I was equipped with underwear riddled with holes, coarse grey trousers and a blue sweater.

I thought I was really tough in those days but looking back I can see how weak I was. I found prison very hard. The loneliness and the nauseating smell of the place depressed me. I kept to myself and thought a lot. I especially thought about Dad. The nights were the worst. The prisoners banged on the doors loudly and for hours just to annoy the warders. Eventually I joined in – it seemed the only way to let off steam and stay sane.

Soon the prison routine felt like the only thing I'd ever known – getting up early, running round the little exercise yard, medicine ball games in the gym which served as a cover for vindictive little scraps between the prisoners. Christmas came and went almost unmarked – it just meant a few more hours in the cell that day, a few more hours to think and feel hopeless. I couldn't even claim to have made any friends. I could see that underneath all the loud talk and bullying the other lads were just as scared and lonely as I was, but I couldn't seem to make the effort to get close to any of them.

All prisons and remand centres have their own little peculiarities – this one had Buchanan. He was a warder with a decidedly strange sense of humour. He used to slide up and down the corridors with dusters under his shoes so that he could creep up on us unawares to see what we were up to!

Dad came once or twice – under pressure from social workers. He didn't know what to say to me, he was worried and fidgety. He told me he'd been going out with a woman, a widow, he said, with lots of money. I didn't really want to know.

I was released after a couple more weeks, then got caught breaking into a café and was sent to a detention centre at Ham Common, near Kingston. Once again found myself caught up in the same tedious and pointless daily routine.

The weekly chapel service was one of my few opportunities to get out of the cell for an hour. The chapel was no more than a prefab hut, with sheets of plastic where the windows should have been. But compared to the prison block it was cosy, and the worn green curtains and dark polished oak chairs were easy on the eye.

The man they called 'padre', he was all right. He had a soft nature and talked in a gentle way, but real all the same. He tried to talk to us about our problems. But we were mostly too scared to take off our masks and admit we could do with some help, me included.

It was a mean, hard time. And each time I got out of prison, life was still hard. I had nowhere to go, nothing to live on and I was often very hungry. For a while I stayed with my patient grandmother in Kingston. My father didn't want to know me. He had married again, this rich woman, and moved into a palatial home in Hampton Court, complete with Rolls Royce, grand piano and swimming pool. I didn't go to the wedding – but the reporters were there in force and I read all about it the next day. 'Fishmonger Marries Ex-Director's Wife' shouted the front page of the Daily Mirror. I tried to visit them, but my father was clearly embarrassed and saw me as a threat to his new lifestyle. He'd become a very rich man overnight. The door was firmly closed on me, with the words 'black sheep' echoing in my ears.

During this time I got engaged – for the second time, though I was still only eighteen. I moved in with Pat, a divorced woman, and her father, who owned a car radiator repair business. He gave me a job in his yard.

The rocky relationship didn't last long. And part of the reason was that I could no longer hide from anyone the fact that I was involved more and more in drinking and taking drugs. I'd first found out about drugs seeing others take them for kicks in a nightclub in Canterbury. Now I started smoking hash (marijuana) myself and soon found if I didn't take it every day I felt really bad.

After I left Pat, I spent months sleeping rough, hiding away in squats or abandoned car wrecks. By night I would break into a café for some food, and then haunt the streets of Piccadilly and Soho looking for the next joint of hash to smoke, the next can of glue to sniff, or the next fix. I hung around with a girl who was a confirmed junkie. The veins in her arms had broken down after years of fixing and she now injected into her feet, and she showed me how to do it too.

Life began to be more like a dream. On drugs I was a victim of horrible visions and shadows, and the line between fantasy and reality blurred and shimmered. Those were the days of the Beatles singing of Eleanor Rigby and 'all those lonely people'. Many people hummed the words. Some, like me, lived them daily.

A search for excitement kept me going. For a time I was obsessed with the idea of becoming a stunt man in films. I had my Army tattoos surgically removed and tracked down the film world, but found – like other worlds I'd briefly visited – that this too was shallow, paper-thin and unsatisfying.

But all the time I didn't lose hope that somewhere, somehow, was something brighter and better than anything I'd found so far. More than anything, I wanted very much to find and belong to a group of sincere human beings. And I thought I'd found the answer when I began to be involved in the Kingston hippy culture. Looking for acceptance, I grew my hair long and began to smoke more and more hash. How could dope be wrong? So it was bad for your health – so what? So was whisky. And cigarettes. Dope made people more friendly, more relaxed. That's how I reasoned with myself, and it all sounded convincing enough at the time. I read books on meditation and spiritualism. I spent hours in well-meaning discussion with students and hippies and felt that maybe at last I was getting somewhere. We talked about peace, self-discovery, truth. And it felt good.

Tired of being hungry and homeless, I began to use my drug-taking contacts as a starting point for what became a lucrative but dangerous business venture. I began to buy large quantities of hash and make them up into 'quid deals'. It was quite profitable, and it honestly never occurred to me that I was making money by exploiting other people's weakness.

I soon found the ideal base for my drug-dealing operation. At a certain pub in Kingston, I discovered there was just one seat in the half-moon-shaped room from which there was a clear view of all three dirty sleazy bars. Jim behind the bar was a big fat ex-policeman who turned a blind eye to the morality behind anything that increased his takings. For the next six years on and off I sat in the same seat in the evenings peddling drugs and making myself a nice big income. With the right tip-offs about the regular police raids, I felt safe enough. I developed a lifestyle that contributed to a certain security. The hippy way of life seemed to make sense to me. How blind I was!

During this period I met several people who had a great deal of influence on me. Two of the most important were Paul and Patsy. Paul was a tree surgeon with the hard, pinched look of a confirmed bad guy – what my father used to call 'a nasty piece of work'! As I got to know him, I realized there was a great deal more to him than his hard appearance, even if he was a very mixed-up guy. He was tall, with short ginger hair. He wore a gold earring in one ear and really way-out clothes. Patsy, the girlfriend over whom he exerted an undoubted masculine dominance, was slim, attractive and artistic. We made an unlikely threesome, but nevertheless became friends and I spent a lot of time in their flat in Surbiton.

I spent a lot of time, too, with Garry, a real Romany, and his friend Ian. I used to go shooting with them, using their hand-made crossbows. One day the three of us went to see a very disturbing documentary film on witchcraft. It featured a man called Alexander who called himself a white witch. And it was the very next day that we went into a record shop – and saw the face of the same Alexander staring at us from a record sleeve.

'It's a sign – we're supposed to buy that record!' I said, excited.

We bought it and went to Garry's flat to play it. It was strange, eerie and hypnotic.

'Turn it off, Garry – it's freaking me out, man!' I said, and Ian said he was going to throw it away, or hide it. But he didn't – and we found we couldn't help listening to it again and again. The record described how to 'invite Satan into the circle'. It was the beginning of a real fascination for me with all things to do with magic and the occult. Repeatedly listening to the record made me feel as if I was in a trance. I began to buy books on black magic and the supernatural, and even asked people if they knew where there was a coven of witches or warlocks meeting. I tried to conduct séances and one night a few of us had a very frightening experience with a ouija board. As we called on Satan, vivid electrical sparks travelled around the room with loud crackling noises. We were terrified by the atmosphere of evil and felt dangerously out of control. We didn't dare use the ouija board again after that.

What with this and the drugs I was taking, it got so that the line between fact and fantasy ceased to exist for me. I looked for the bizarre in all that happened and often found it. I wanted more and more of the whole hippie and drug culture. Surely if I got in deeper and deeper I would get more and more meaning out of life, more and more satisfaction? Maybe this was the start of something exciting for me, or so I told myself. Organised religion turned me off – but surely there had to be more to life than what was on the surface. Was this the route – through drugs and meditation to spiritualism, magic, Eastern philosophy – to the ultimate truths of life? I wasn't going to give up until I'd discovered the secret of it all.

Deep down this all made me feel even more restless. And so when two of my hippy friends, Cliff and his girlfriend Laura, announced they were off to India, home of the hash farms, the mysterious East that drew all hippies, I didn't hesitate.

'I'm coming with you – when do we leave?' I said.

This was it – a great adventure that promised to take me in the right direction towards what I was really searching for in life!

CHAPTER 2

It was going to be a tight squeeze! In the van there would be Cliff, Laura and Jamie, their blond two-year-old son. Gus. And me.

Cliff was the shrewd planner behind the trip. An ex-private schoolboy, he closely resembled a gypsy. He had curly mouse-coloured hair and beard, with dark rings under his deep-set eyes. His American girlfriend Laura was an intelligent, strong-willed girl with long ginger hair and a freckled face. Gus was altogether a strange guy, thin and stooping, with pointed nose, bulging eyes and short black greasy hair. Not the most 'together' of people, but he did know about mechanics and was supplying the old Bedford van we were using to take us off on our adventure.

India – land of mystery! I'd been to parts of Europe with the Army and Merchant Navy, but this was something else. We spread the maps out and plotted the route. First to Calais... then from France to Switzerland, Germany, Italy, Austria, Yugoslavia, Greece, Turkey, Syria, Iraq, Iran, Afghanistan, Pakistan and India. Just saying the names of the countries out loud seemed mysterious. We would speed through Europe as quickly as possible to Turkey and those other Eastern countries where hash was cheap and easily available.

We set our leaving date for the end of July. That meant just a few weeks to raise the cash each of us would need for the early stages of the journey – about £150 each. This was no real bother to me. My 'income' through my position as local drug dealer was assured. Trade was brisk and I could count on selling about £80 worth of drugs on a good night, the return on about £20 worth of hash I'd bought and made up into small 'quid deals'.

I made arrangements for Ian and Garry to take over my drug contacts and keep business ticking over while I was away. Soon I was ready and impatient for the leaving date to come.

I wasn't so sorry to be leaving it all behind, I began to think to myself. Sure, it was exciting, sitting there in the darkened room of the pub every night. I always got there at opening time to be sure of my own seat from which I was guaranteed a clear view of everyone coming and going. As the hours wore on, the disco lights would flash brighter and the music boom louder. Dealing was a highly complex game. I enjoyed drugs and enjoyed turning other people on. But if the excitement was always there – so was the fear. Like a fast-flowing river with treacherous undercurrents, it threatened to erode the banks of reason and carry me away to the rapids. Sometimes my own heartbeat pulsed louder than the music as I slunk away through the side door and down the back lanes whenever the alarm was raised – 'Quick, Terry mate – coppers' raid!'

And during the last few days before our departure there was one incident in particular which shook my confidence in the way I'd been living. A big guy aged about twenty came to deal from Norwich. He bought a lot of drugs. The arrangement was that I should follow him by car to a house to pick up the money. As soon as we were on the edge of London he put his foot down and roared off. I was so angry at this blatant deceit I hardly knew what I was doing. Honour among thieves? It seemed not. In a rage, I raced home, got a knife and went round to Paul's flat. I told him what had happened and we both jumped into his old Mini pickup and set off, driving through the night and arriving in Norwich in the early hours.

It didn't take us long to make contact with some local addicts and they told us where our man was living. We soon tracked him down to his squat, a derelict house in a depressing dark back street. It was a spooky place, made even spookier when we came across my so-called friend lying asleep in a huge box that looked just like a coffin. I'm afraid, big as he was, I roughed him up a bit. And I got my stuff back – it was hidden in a hole in the ceiling. As we drove home my anger gave way to bitterness and depression. Was there anyone I could really trust? Was everyone motivated deep down by selfishness and greed? After all, when it came to the crunch, I had been. So many of my hippy friends seemed peaceful, even gentle. Was all this talk of 'make love not war' and 'flower power' just another cheap veneer under which lurked the same soiled human nature I saw all around me?

The question hung over me like a stubborn black cloud, threatening the apparent ease of the life I'd been living now for several years. But I packed my bag and packed away the problem, too. I wasn't going to let anything spoil my great adventure – the trip to India.

For the next few months, I and my travelling companions lived just a day at a time and the freedom was exhilarating. We travelled, we marvelled, we talked for hours, we slept under the stars, we ate whenever and whatever we liked. We camped in the Black Forest and walked through miles of fir trees and pebbled forest floors. The turreted fairy-tale castles and green landscapes, the rushing rivers, the amazing variety of all that we saw, took words and breath away. It was a clean fresh world that made the rainy black streets of London a vaguely remembered dream that was losing its power.

In one Yugoslavian village we were drawn by the sounds of lively music, singing and clapping. Inside a hall dozens of people were drinking heartily, dancing in laughing circles and playing concertinas. In spite of the suspicious frowns of the older villagers we joined in the celebrations too!

That was one of many happy incidents that to this day have created in me a mental 'picture diary' of those travels. Whenever I think of Bulgaria, for example, I see a smiling band of over twenty Romany gypsies, the gold of their earrings and brightness of their clothes matched only by the gaudy painted colours of their caravans. Further along the same steeply banked road we met children leading great bears by ropes tied to rings through their noses. The children played tambourines and held out begging bowls as the bears performed their comical dance.

Another picture I have is of little Jamie dancing on a platform in a café in Greece to a blaring juke box. Behind him, through the doorway, the clear blue waters of the Mediterranean played with the masses of tiny pebbles on the beach.

We got to Turkey before our own supply of hash

began to run out. The café owners in Istanbul didn't seem at all shocked or even surprised when we asked them where we could get some. They pointed up the road – to the east, where not too far away now we could see the snow-capped peak of Mount Ararat.

As we neared the Turkish border with Iraq there was a strange sense of threatening which steadily increased. We were nervous, as we'd heard stories of an American girl being shot there recently for carrying LSD. Imagine our utter amazement when the Turkish ambassador and an Army official invited us into the Customs building and offered us beds for the night and asked if we wanted to smoke hash! We swallowed hard and refused, desperately trying to keep the conversation light and relaxed. We suspected that they were trying to lay a trap for us.

They let us through the barriers and we breathed deep sighs of relief. The road we took was now well off the main tourist track. We passed through little settlements where people wrapped in rags peered listlessly at us from the doorways of their dirt-floored huts. There was squalor and poverty all around, and a strange heavy atmosphere of oppression and mistrust.

Beyond Mount Ararat a flat billiard table of land stretched for miles and miles. One morning as we set off, a very fine rain began to fall and the wind started to howl. Soon the rain hardened and it was gusting so badly we could make hardly any progress in our van over the mud and boulders. The roaring wind tore at the van doors until they were both flung open like wings. As we struggled to pull them in again the luggage was snatched from the roof rack and sent hurtling into a ditch. We retrieved it and pressed on, barely making ten miles an hour over the rough terrain.

Finally we came to a definite halt. The left front wheel was completely seized up. Cliff, Gus and I got out, leaving Laura – now heavily pregnant – inside with little Jamie, who was crying miserably. We spread a huge sheet of thick polythene over the seized wheel and crawled under it with our bag of tools to see if we could fix it.

Suddenly the sounds of high-pitched yells, wild shouting and the thundering of horses' hooves reached us. We got to our feet and strained our eyes through the gloom to see what new anxiety was coming our way. What we saw was rather like a scene from a film – only not nearly so comfortable, as all this was frighteningly real. Out of the slanting grey drizzle appeared four men on horseback waving rifles. They were Kurdish tribesmen. They pulled up, still jeering loudly, just feet from us. They were all dark skinned and wild eyed. They wore baggy peasant trousers and leather boots and there were full bullet belts crossed over their heaving chests. The horses trod the ground impatiently – their mouths, I noticed, were torn and bleeding and their flanks sweaty and quivering. We stood, hardly daring to move, while they looked us over, spitting, flicking their whips and making sounds like groans and curses in their unintelligible language. Two of them began to circle us and the van, two peered in through the windows. One stared at me, his eyes unblinking and his face like granite. I stared back, and it seemed for several minutes we held each other unmoving with our eyes meeting like that.

'Cliff,' I said quietly, trying to keep my voice firm. My eyes still held the man nearest me.

'Cliff, we'd better give them something. That's what they want.'

The next thing that happened was so unpredictable and terrifying that even in the split second that it occurred I began to prepare myself mentally for death.

Driven by fear or stupidity – I'm not sure which – Cliff drew a packet of fifty tiny foreign cigarettes out of his trouser pocket and threw them at one of the tribesman. The packet landed with a little slap on his lap, and the cigarettes spilt out everywhere.

'You mad or something!' I hissed. 'They'll kill you for an insult like that! They'll kill us all!'

But no... without warning, as if by some unspoken agreement, all four turned their horses' heads silently and galloped off. We stood staring after them, not daring to believe they had gone, and certainly not understanding why.

Within a short time Cliff and Gus were able to congratulate themselves for getting out of the desperate situation and to minimise the fear they'd experienced. Such is human nature. As for me, though, I was not ashamed to confess how shaken I was and how incomprehensible it was to me that I was still alive. The eyes of the tribesman stayed with me. And I admitted to myself that my own interpretation of what happened that day was quite different to what the others had experienced. You see, I felt very definitely that we had been protected by some invisible presence. It seemed to me that an invisible barrier had just suddenly dropped down between us and the tribesmen. I couldn't talk about it to the others. Not only did I realise that they did not share my feelings about the episode but I knew it sounded pretty foolish.

After several more hours struggling with the wheel, we gave up. We took what we could carry of our luggage in backpacks and set off on foot through the inhospitable landscape towards the nearest Iraqi village. Fortunately, after a few miles we were able to hitch a lift in the back of an open truck.

But things got tougher from then on. Inevitably progress was slower without the van and this aggravated the growing tension between the four of us. It wasn't easy for us to have a break from each other and the friction was almost tangible at times. But the momentum of the need to get hash pushed us onwards. Anyway, if we stopped life was even more difficult. The people were surly; they turned their eyes away from us and crossed the streets to avoid us. If we paused to look in a shop window, policemen would appear from nowhere and come alongside, jostling us, telling us to move on.

We stayed in some pretty rough places, in villages that were no more than a row of shacks, mostly made of mud daubed on to wooden props. One day we hitched a lift into one of these countless nameless places and easily spotted the hotel as the only two-storey building there. Inside, we stood at the bottom of a flight of stairs looking around. Eventually a grinning face appeared in a doorway and a lethargic figure slowly eased himself into the room.

'Yessah?'

His turban was ridiculously unraveled right down to the ground but he didn't seem to notice. We asked to see the manager and he pointed to a room behind the desk. We knocked at the glass-panelled door and went in. The manager himself contributed greatly to the comic air of the place. Even in the sweltering heat he wore a big black hat, black suit, white shirt and black tie. He fanned his glistening face, his huge shiny nose and his tiny neat moustache, also black, with a sheaf of papers. Which one of the Marx brothers was he?

'Can you tell us the time of the next bus out of here?' we asked.

This guy was a real joker and it was two hours before we stumbled out of the room, laughing hysterically ourselves and with his insane giggling still echoing in our ears.

Time and again we were to find such amazingly original characters tucked away in these remote places. Perhaps it was just that he saw so few people come his way. Trying to mislead, delay and entertain those he did see was obviously all he lived for! However, when we'd stopped laughing at his comical antics and sign-language jokes, we found we didn't feel quite so amused. The next bus out of town wasn't for another five days!

We booked rooms there for the equivalent of two and a half pence per night each. Sounds cheap, but believe me, we were overcharged! Lizards crawled up the grubby walls and bed bugs infested the thin mattresses. The wooden framed beds had a few ropes for springs.

We were heading next for the road to the Khyber Pass – reckoned as being a good place for dope. We were travelling pretty light by now – no van and we'd been selling off bits of our luggage en route to pay our way. We did some pretty good deals, though. We discovered what many tourists regularly took advantage of – that the local people would pay vastly inflated prices for literally anything Western.

In between hitching rides and taking jolting bus journeys, we spent long hours in the village 'chi houses'. We would enter these mud huts, having first followed the custom of removing our shoes, and mount a carpeted platform to sit, drink tea and smoke hash from what we called 'bubble pipes'.

These were good times. I loved to sit and chat philosophically to the local old men in the chi houses. I felt I was getting a deeper understanding of the meaning of life from these sincere old men. Unlike their children, they weren't worshipping and coveting all things Western. They preserved a more ancient way of life and were content with it. I had some fascinating conversations with them.

I loved to wander through the medinas – the bustling Eastern market-places. The noise, the smells and the closeness of the people were all intoxicatingly exciting to me. I watched the native cobblers at work, the shrivelled old men sitting cross-legged selling incense and herbs, other stallholders dyeing their merchandise in huge sunken holes in the ground. A cloud of dust would announce the arrival of a train of mules, the driver waving them on through the narrow cobbled streets with yells and prods of his stick.

It was at one of these many little markets in the capital Kabul that we all bought the padded and embroidered waistcoats we took to wearing. I bought a thick green one with lots of pockets and elaborate embroidery, as well as tiny mirrors sewn into it. I decided to buy a second, undid some of the seams and exchanged some of the padding material for hash. This I parcelled up and sent back to Ian and Garry in England, for which they returned some much-needed cash to me. It was a risky business – post office officials were always on the lookout for this sort of thing, but later I sent back another jacket stuffed with hash, and on another occasion even a large jar of cocaine, and got away with it.

Coming out of Kabul, we headed along the main route towards the Khyber Pass. At the roadside local people were skinning goats to take to the medinas, and below us stretched away plains dotted with scattered interruptions of rock piles. Occasionally we passed a group of Bedouin tents and caught glimpses of the Bedouin women at work in their beautifully embroidered bright red and purple gowns.

Life settled down for a few weeks when in one of the many small settlements along the way Cliff bumped into an Englishman he knew called Guy. Guy invited us to stay in his house, a sort of mud castle with a large courtyard overlooking the lovely Afghanistan hills. The beauty of the surroundings compensated for the primitive lifestyle. There were no toilet or washing facilities and at night, when the temperature always fell dramatically, the only heating was an open fire fed by pancakes of dried donkey dung.

After a couple of days, Guy went away on some moneymaking business expedition in Lahore, trading horses. Left to ourselves, we held unending parties, inviting people in and heating up large lumps of hash in a red-hot frying pan on Guy's gas cooker. Sometimes these evenings were so intense I found I had lain in a stupor or totally unconscious for hours on the floor, awaking cramped and freezing cold in the grey morning light.

Now that the routine of travelling began to wear off a little, I was more aware than ever of the tension between Cliff, Laura, Gus and myself. I took to spending as much of the time as possible on my own, often sitting up in the hills. And a terrible loneliness began to hurt deep inside.

My depression intensified when I began to feel very ill, with long bouts of vomiting and crippling stomach pains. The local chemist could offer me nothing but cocaine. After several weeks I was weak and exhausted. I felt desperate for home and rosily-remembered friends.

One day, sitting as I often did alone in the hills, I thought about London and about Paul and Patsy, my hippie friends in Surbiton. I stroked the silver Christ on the large wooden cross I now always wore around my neck. It had been a parting gift from Paul and touching it was a sort of comfort to me. I decided I would go home. But not without some hash. I began to make my plans as carefully as my tired wits would allow.

Back at the house I told the others my news. Gus was going to stay on here. So would Cliff and Laura for a while, then they planned to work their way home overland. They wanted to take some of the beautiful Afghani carpets with them to sell in England.

Later that evening I stared at my reflection in an old mirror. With long, unkempt hair and an unshaven face, I looked ill in spite of the tan. As usual I was wearing old sandals on my bare feet, baggy Eastern-style trousers and my well-worn green embroidered waistcoat over an old yellow t-shirt. No, it wouldn't do, not if I was to succeed in my plan. Looking like this I'd be searched immediately for drugs solely on the grounds of my appearance.

I knew I'd have to make some fairly drastic improvements. First, I bought some straight Western-style trousers, proper shoes and a real shirt. With a shave and a close haircut, I began to look more like the average tourist.

I said a few farewells and boarded the bus. First stop – Pakistan. The journey, six agonising weeks on a succession of ancient jolting buses, was a nightmare. All I could get to drink was Coke, which I drank to try to cope with my raging thirst, but it made me violently sick. Not the most useful thing to happen when I was trying to act inconspicuous! I felt dizzy and knew I was losing a lot of weight. I seemed to have no strength at all left in my entire body.

In my low state I was terrified I would be found out for the five kilos of hash I was carrying in the bottom of my case. I could smell it all the time and worried that others would notice it. I kept scenting it with talcum powder.

One day I was grateful when we reached an oasis near Peshawar and I could have a short break from the bumpy bus ride. I was so feverish and ill, I felt for the first time like really giving up. Giving up what? Well, life itself. It didn't seem worth living right now.

I sat on the edge of the well overshadowed by a clump of palm trees. It was a deep well. Just suppose I was to lean over just a bit too far and...

'Excuse me... If you would be so kind. I'd like to get a drink.'

I stared up into the first new white face I'd seen for months. A friendly white face at that. He was a young German, tall and blond. I moved aside to let him drink some of the well water and he gave some to me. It tasted good, surprisingly cool. The simple act of kindness somehow lifted my spirit. And as I sipped it and listened to the boy's animated conversion I began to feel more alive. I could make it. I could. I mustn't give up now. Not while there was just this shred of hope left in me.

I felt little better by the time I got to Rawalpindi in Pakistan. I booked into a neat clean little hotel near the station and prepared myself mentally for the next stage of my plan.

'So you see, sir, that's exactly how it happened! I know I should have been more careful. The worst thing was losing everything in one go – clothes, my camera, all my holiday money, stolen like that. I guess you must get really fed up with us tourists!'

The embassy official grunted and went back to scribbling in the forms.

'Just look in at the embassy in a few days, Mr. Jarvis.'

He dismissed me with the curt little nod he saved for all careless tourists who should know better.

I left feeling better than I had done for weeks. Almost elated. In fact it was several weeks and many trips to the embassy, all the time worrying about the hash I was carrying, but eventually I was given the news I was waiting for. I was being repatriated. I was on my way home!

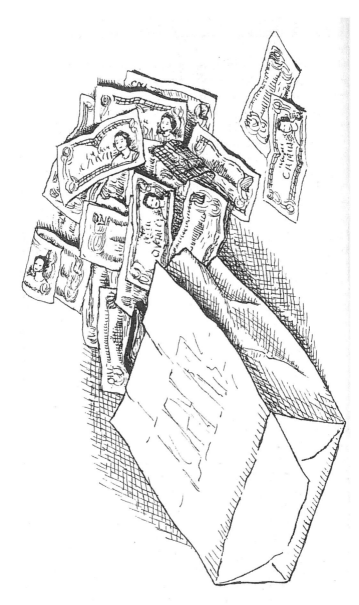

CHAPTER 3

P redictably, it was raining when the plane touched down at Heathrow. My stomach was knotted as hard as iron and my mouth was dry. I knew I had to play and win the psychological victory game if I wanted to walk out through Customs with those five kilos of hash in the false bottom of my suitcase. I was satisfied my costume was right for the part. But when the cue came, that wouldn't be enough – I'd have to be word perfect, too. They say a good actor lives and believes his part. I summoned every ounce of concentration I possessed to carry off my performance. After all, there was only one show, one chance to get it right. And if it was a flop it wouldn't mean a slow hand clap or a barrage of rotten eggs – but a prison sentence!

Ahead of me in the line, slowly inching past the desks, were half a dozen Indians. I hated to do it, but I had to use them as stage props. I read the contempt in the eyes of the Customs officers. 'Why can't you go back home where you belong?' they seemed to say. As I waited my turn, I copied the same coldness of eye, the same sneering, thin-lipped looks those officers had. I'd have to submerge my real feeling for these Indians for the next few minutes. My freedom depended on mentally lining myself up on the same side as those Customs officers.

I feigned impatience, huffing and puffing, shuffling my feet and drumming my fingers on the desk over the delay as the officers searched the bags of the last two or three Indians in front of me.

My turn. I brought my hand down hard on the lid of my suitcase with a thump that made everyone turn round.

'At long last! Now, look here. I think I ought to report this matter to someone in authority. Just look at the damage done to my suitcase. See, this split here, and this other one here? Ruined! Holiday! That's a laugh! First some Paki runs off with every penny I've got, leaving me stranded. And when I finally get home – weeks late – what do I find? On the way, wonderful British Airways has ripped my case to pieces!'

A few more loud and contemptuous criticisms of the flight and they couldn't wait to get rid of me! Well done, Terry, you deserve an Oscar! I told myself with relief as I strolled through the carpeted lounge. The sight of a police Land Rover parked outside the big glass windows checked my enthusiasm. It wasn't over yet. I couldn't afford to take any chances.

Taking care to see I wasn't being followed from the airport, I made my way to a piece of desolate scrapland I knew along the Great South West Road leading out of London. It was a place where I'd once worked for a while for a man called Greg.

It was dusk as I picked my way over the site. In the distance I saw dimly the faint outline of the caravan office and beyond that the two garages with up-and-over doors. The wasteland immediately in front of me was littered with the rusting shells of cars with the innards gone or spilling out, and heaps of abandoned machinery and broken furniture.

The wind rattled through bits of corrugated iron

and made me jumpy. I felt all the time that I was being followed and kept looking back over my shoulder.

Near a sagging bed frame propped against an old tree stump, I broke off a piece from a plank of wood and started to dig a hole with it in the ground. It was hard going, the earth was solid. When eventually I'd dug a narrow hole reaching down about a foot I transferred all the little plastic bags of hash from my suitcase into the hole and filled it in again. Then, wiping my hands as well as I could, I headed for the caravan office. The site looked empty but I could hear scraping sounds from the nearby garages so guessed the men were still at work there.

'Hey, Greg! You at home?'

The mean scheming face of my former boss appeared first at the window and then around the door.

'Terry, old son! What brings you round these parts again? I heard you was out of the country.'

Greg's welcome was not sincere. And it was short-lived. No, he did not want to be in on any drug deal. He would stick to bank hold-ups and blue movies, thanks. That was what he knew best.

Definitely no deal, there. I'd just have to get rid of the hash my own way. I had been hopeful he'd give me a lift into Kingston – my nerves were in a bit of a delicate state and I wasn't sure I could face going on the bus. Still, now I had no choice. I walked back to the main road and caught the bus.

It was good to see everyone again. I went to stay with Garry and Ian and was soon at home with the old crowd. After a couple of days I dug up the hash and took it back to the flat. But I hadn't forgotten the trust problem. I just couldn't let it out of my sight.

The load was worth thousands of pounds. Word soon got around and attempts were made to steal it. And these were the people I called friends! I soon felt my longing to be back had been misplaced. I couldn't even trust Garry and Ian not to help themselves to some of the hash. Not only was there the constant anxiety of watching over it, knowing that if I let my guard down the temptation would prove too much for someone, but there was the worry of finding the right contacts through which to dispose of large quantities of the drug and make a good profit on the deal.

When I'd been back home a few months, news reached me that Cliff and Laura had got into trouble – and out again! The baby Laura had been expecting had arrived safely. But apparently Cliff and Guy had been caught red-handed in a stolen van carrying a load of hash in Afghanistan somewhere. The hash had belonged to Cliff and Laura – but Guy had spoken up and said it was his. And they'd obviously let him take the whole rap.

Guy was given a twelve-year prison sentence! I felt sick when I heard about it, remembering some of the appalling prisons I'd seen in Iran, which were no more than barbaric torture dungeons. I felt I never wanted to see Cliff and Laura again.

Time to think hard. I had made a lot of money selling the hash, more than enough to live comfortably on for about a year without working. But now that the initial relief of being back home, getting rid of the stuff and being on the mend as far as my health was concerned had worn off, it seemed to me that life had never been grayer. I was aware that all the promise of my trip to India had not really materialised, but I was still certain that there was much more of the Eastern way of life that I had yet to discover. So, when the money did begin to get low it seemed natural to invest what there was left into another drug trip. This time I'd go direct to Pakistan – by air.

Experience was teaching me how careful I needed to be in both leaving and entering a country. I applied for another passport and filled in the application as a 'student of philosophy'. When I went to get the passport photos taken I had my hair cut short and padded out my cheeks with wads of cotton wool. My face would need to look chubbier than it naturally was to appear in proportion to what I had planned for the rest of me – the corset. I bought an ordinary corset which fitted around my whole trunk from just under my arms. With a few careful alterations and additions it became a purpose-built hash-smuggling belt. It was ideal for the job – though not, as I was to discover, the most comfortable of garments!

Corseted, cotton wool padded and respectable-looking, I landed a few weeks later at Karachi. Like most other Europeans at the airport I was besieged by swarms of skinny dark children and men who pulled at my sleeves, begging and inviting, 'Want hashish, mister? Want hashish, follow? Hashish, come?' But these weren't the kind of contacts I wanted to make and the airport lounge wasn't the place to be seen taking an interest in such invitations.

I booked into a modest hotel in Rawalpindi. The next two weeks I spent making contacts in the chi houses and in the dark alleys behind the bars. The humid town streets were alive, even at three o'clock in the morning, with beggars and stalls still selling their wares. Often I would come across small groups of people gathered around fires on the roadsides, smoking and talking together. They would make a terrific fuss of any Westerners they saw, and many of them would call me over to join them, putting their arms around me as a token that they wanted to be friends. Many of the stallholders who beckoned me were crippled people who lived on the few coins they could beg. I discovered that some of them had been deliberately crippled and maimed by their parents so that they could earn money for the family by begging. One man I often saw on my late walks was a tiny middle-aged dwarf. He was a grey-haired and moustached miniature, only about two feet tall. He would spread out a hankie in front of him for people to put money on, and alongside it were three brass cans with burning rags in.

I spent a lot of time alone, too, and after the strain of life in London found a terrific relaxation in being so free to think. There were a few other Westerners around – tourists or hippies living in a commune on the beach. But most of the time I spent alone, wandering on the edge of the desert or by the brilliantly blue sea.

One day in my solitary wanderings I discovered a huge overturned turtle shell lying in a gash in the rocks on a lonely stretch of beach. The local villagers had obviously killed the turtle for its meat. It was wonderful, huge – about six feet across – and beautifully marked. The shell had been robbed of its life, the turtle body ripped out greedily. But there, nestling up against the dead shell, were clusters of jelly eggs, hundreds of them, prematurely exposed, never to know birth.

I stared at it for a long, long time, caressing the shell

with my hand. I wanted to get some meaning out of the cruelty of it, the life and death of it. The horror of it held me, the beauty of it attracted me so much my thoughts ran over and over again on ways in which I could possess and use the shell.

Like the abused shell, life and death seemed exposed in this country. The sun beat down, penetrating into the skin of everything. There was no hiding. The sun shone into me and exposed my thoughts and questions. Here, as nowhere else, there was an urgency to find answers. But none seemed to come. On one of my long walks I passed always at the same spot the same naked old man sitting on the edge of the dusty track. He was always there, just sitting and thinking, living. Why? Was he finding answers? What sense was he making of his existence? To suffer the indignity of his position without apparent awareness like that, did he know something I did not? Did he want something I did not? Certainly the unblinking serenity of his dark, aboriginal-like face was other-worldly.

Near the old man's inert dusty body was a temple. A long run of steps led up to a tomb, guarded day and night. Some highly enlightened person, I was told, was being remembered, his life being perpetuated in the reverence of his followers. At the foot of the steps there was a parade of stalls selling clay bangles, incense and beautiful cut flowers. The dead prophet slept beside the bustle of the daily trading. Life and death seemed to overlap, or even to be the same thing to these people. Alongside the old prophet or the raucous street traders or the dusty old man sitting in his oblivion, I felt I was a shadow, a man without answers or reasons for being.

In between my long walks I would drink tea and occasionally smoke hash at the little chi houses, mostly shacks on the beach made of bamboo and woven matting. One day I lay in the sun for hours but back at the hotel my face became so swollen and painful I could barely open my eyes and was forced to lie in the relative cool of my room for the whole of the next day to recover.

Finally, I found the right contacts, made my deal and after some time a bundle of hash was delivered to me and carefully squeezed in little polythene bags into the many pockets of my special corset. So it was time to return to England. I got into my 'straight' outfit – slim-fitting trousers, shirt, tie, jacket, even an overcoat to drape over my arm! – and checked out of the hotel.

Going through Customs, just yards from the metal detector I remembered with horror that a strategically placed safety pin might give me away. Trying to keep calm, I dropped out of the queue as casually as possible and made my way to the toilets – to remove the metal pin which secured the bandage holding the top of my corset in place.

The rest of the seventeen-hour journey home passed without incident but not without a great deal of personal agony. The corset, now stiff with the packets of hash, was like a straitjacket and the bottom edge of it cut painfully into the tops of my legs.

Back home, I returned to trading from my old seat at the Kingston pub with a profitable supply of hash, enough to last for some time. But it wasn't long before I was troubled with the familiar dissatisfaction with my way of life and with the shallow people around me.

Deep down there was a longing that drugs or drug dealing or the hippy way of life did not touch. And, anyway, trade did not seem as brisk as it had been.

I was told that I could get a much better price for what I was selling in Canada. There seemed no reason at all to hesitate about going there. Not surprisingly, smuggling via a corset had lost its appeal! But Toronto Customs had the reputation of being especially tough to get through. So I hit on another plan. I'd got to know a young guy called Dean whose father actually worked at Heathrow Airport. He was a drug user himself, but managed not to let it show. He was pretty straight-looking, neat and quiet. He jumped at the chance of earning a couple of hundred pounds by carrying the stuff for me from Heathrow to Toronto. We got hold of a false-bottomed suitcase for him to use, hid the stuff in it and arranged that we would go separately to the airport and meet up on board the plane.

It soon became apparent that Dean was not quite as cool as he looked! By the time we were halfway over the Atlantic he'd worked himself up into a highly nervous and agitated state that was so obvious that it was as much as I could do to keep my head myself.

'Terry, the deal's off. I can't go through with it! I just can't, I know I'll get caught. You can have your money back, every penny, honest! But I can't, Terry, I just can't do it.'

He passed one shaking hand over his white face and gripped my arm with the other. I was aware that at any time the stewardess or any of the other passengers might wonder about his urgent whispers and odd looks.

'Calm down, Dean! Take it easy! No hassle, it'll be

perfectly all right as long as you keep your cool. We've got to go through with it now. There's no turning back. You got that? Just take it easy.'

I tried to ignore him, staring hard out of the window.

At Toronto Airport I strode ahead, leaving him to it. He'd have to get through somehow. And if he didn't, I couldn't afford to be standing next to him.

Pale and still trembling, he finally appeared through the barrier and we got into a taxi. Now the worst of the danger was over I exploded with anger. I told him just what I thought of his pathetic performance. He didn't retaliate, just cowered in the corner of the taxi like a schoolboy who'd just been caned.

Our taxi dropped us off at the apartment building in the centre of Toronto where we were due to meet our first contact, a guy called Keith. Keith answered the door wearing a surprising pastel blue velvet catsuit that made me cringe with embarrassment! As we introduced ourselves I noticed there was another occupant of the flat – a beautiful brown-skinned girl with long hair tied back in a pony tail who flitted in and out of the room. Keith didn't mention who she was.

Dean and I moved into their front room and set about dealing with the network of contacts we met through Keith, trying to negotiate the best price possible for the hash we'd brought with us. After screening, I eventually got an audience with one of the top drug men in the city. This involved being checked out by a team of muscled heavies in the reception area of a twelve-storey block, and watched by banks of TV monitors until we were allowed upstairs to meet the head man. The whole building, in the heart of the student quarter of Toronto, had been taken over by the drug ring. However, these guys were far too greedy – they wanted my drugs at a giveaway price but I refused. And some days later I managed to conclude a much better deal with another contact.

After agreeing on a final price, I rushed back to my room to check on the hash. I couldn't trust Dean not to have taken some of it. He'd become a real responsibility to have around, so jumpy and careless I knew I had to stick close to him, at least until the drugs were handed over. I inspected the drugs I'd packed into a holdall. The hash was over-dry when we'd arrived in Canada so I'd damped it down. Now I took it up on the roof to dry it out a little, then cut and weigh it. I wrapped the little black crumbly cubes individually in foil. They looked just like stock cubes – but were nowhere near as innocent!

I got paid in dollars. It was a great deal of money. Rather foolishly I stuffed it all into a carrier bag, took it to a nearby bank and converted it all into traveller's cheques. But no one questioned me.

We decided to hang around for a few weeks before going home. But now that the trading was over, life was becoming boring. At least, it was for me. Dean had got himself involved with a group of guys in the next-door flat who were 'fixing' – injecting drugs, heroin and morphine mostly. I knew how terribly dangerous mainlining was and often told him how crazy he was. But then one day when I was feeling very low, Dean persuaded me to go next door with him. In the bedroom it was warm and the music was loud. Five or six people lay on cushions smoking and talking. They didn't seem such a bad crowd after all, and I was lonely that day. Dean started mixing up a heaped teaspoon of heroin – a massive dose. I refused to take it from him, but he was very persuasive and before I'd had time to think about it I'd let him inject me with it.

Within minutes my whole body was transformed into a simmering volcano. I was drowning in the hot lava, it washed over me in violent waves. Huge air bubbles rose up through my volcano body to burst in the seething crater that was my head. I was massive, all-powerful. I was an alien. I was a living, moving, magnificent volcano. Strength and ecstasy that was agony surged through me. Never before, never, had I felt that good. I flew, I floated, I bathed in the lava.

Then the volcano erupted. My head was bursting apart. I rushed across the room. I needed to hold on to something to stop the force ripping me apart. My body was charging about with an energy I couldn't control. I took a grip on the window sill and as I grabbed it my feet nearly touched the ceiling and vomit shot out into the street. Drugged, dazed, walking in another world, I staggered next door to Keith's room.

There I found no one but the beautiful brown-skinned girl. I needed to talk, to express the depth and meaning of this new experience. And she was there and she listened. She was lovely. A smooth slim body, long dark hair and large brown knowing eyes. She understood. She cared. We talked through the night and the dawn found us lovers. I hungered for more heroin with a longing that frightened me. I wanted to go back next door, to inject again, to relive that volcano pleasure that was calling me desperately. It was a craving I'd never known before. But Christiana wouldn't let me go. She knew I stood at the threshold of madness and horror and she wouldn't let me go. I longed, I craved, I was mad. But she reasoned, she talked, she loved. And she wouldn't let me go.

The hours passed. The brightness of the new day began to filter through the curtains. The hold of the drug experience began to weaken and my love for her to grow. She had truly saved me that night.

CHAPTER 4

Finding Christiana was like opening a door on a whole new chapter in my life. None of the fleeting relationships I'd had with girls before had ever been like this magical closeness. A French-Algerian, at twenty-seven Christiana was seven years older than me. She had been a professional ballet dancer and was fighting to resume her career after a hurtful relationship with Keith which had ended in an abortion a few months before we met. She was working hard, training in expression dancing and her aim was to teach dancing in Vancouver.

I loved her vitality and her bright mind, and I felt I wanted to be with her always. With the drug deals complete, I had made several thousand dollars. Over the past three or four years I'd made in total about £18,000 in English money, one way and another. We made plans together for a shared future.

In the months that followed we were increasingly happy with each other. We led a comfortable life and travelled a lot. I felt that in many respects I was happier than I ever had been. I had achieved something, got somewhere, and I was loved and in love. It was a far cry from being hungry and homeless in London, or desolate and forgotten behind the prison bars of some nameless institutions.

Yet… There was still a 'yet'! Somehow deep inside there was a gap in that satisfaction, a hole in that contentment I couldn't define. I talked it over with Christiana and she said she recognised a missing 'something' in her life, too. She suggested we should explore yoga and meditation in our search for answers. I remembered how with Ian and Garry I'd investigated the occult and black magic. I'd hovered on the fringe of yoga and meditation and felt it had real value to the searching person. Perhaps now was the time to go deeper and find those elusive answers. We started going to evening classes run by a Japanese man who was a serene-faced yogi master by night and a smiling postman by day.

We became keen and serious students of the yoga vision. We learned of the philosophy of tapping our inner powers, finding resources lying dormant within and bringing them into use. Staring at the focus of a candle flame we disciplined our minds, purged them, refined them. Every morning we were faithful to the ritual chant – 'Ummmm…' – which we were told was the first sound made by man. Those involved in meditation believe that in making that chant they are restored to a right communication with the Creator and will then have peace of mind. My dedication to yoga extended beyond daily rituals of meditation and chanting to intensive study of Eastern religions which involved such rites. I read keenly, devouring information.

After we'd been together for a few months Christiana's sixteen-year-old brother Pierre came over from Marseilles to stay with us. Life was difficult during that time. He spoke no English and expected Christiana to devote all her time to showing him around. She had a very strong attachment to her family and I could see that she was under a lot of pressure to return to them in France. Seeing how torn she was, I tried to convince her that it would be a good idea to come to England with me for a three-month visit, and she finally gave in to my persuasion.

In England that summer we paired up with a friend in Surbiton, Philip, and his Swedish girlfriend. He was deeply involved in sun worship. Big yellow suns were embroidered on his Indian-style clothes to bear witness to it. He intrigued me and I was fascinated by his sense of freedom. Sometimes for fun I would ask him to do his sun dance and we'd laugh to see him whooping and prancing around like a North American Indian. We often went to Richmond Park together and, lying on the parched grass, we would talk long and deep about life as we saw it.

Staring up at the blue sky one day he said to me, 'Terry, I shall be glad when I go home.' I knew exactly what he meant.

'Me, too,' I replied earnestly. I meant it, too. We were serious; it was a completely solemn moment for us. We didn't feel of this world. Philip told me about his plans to get a commune together to live on Dartmoor. I don't think he ever succeeded – and a year or two later I heard he'd died of an overdose.

I took Christiana to visit all my other friends in London – including, of course, Paul and Patsy, who didn't seem to have changed much.

Then, to please Christiana, we went to Marseilles to visit her family. As I'd half expected, I found the whole family difficult to be with. Pierre insisted on following us around, and there never seemed to be much to do. We spent a lot of time on hired mopeds exploring the dirty rocky coastline. Or we took off into the caves in the hills to sit for hours and meditate. But I didn't really like it there and finally we agreed to separate for a few weeks – Christiana would stay on with her family for a bit longer and I would return to England. Then we would meet up to emigrate to Canada for good.

Back in London I went to stay with Paul and Patsy for a while and then moved into a bedsit at the rear of a large converted mansion. It was a long, narrow, white-painted room with a verandah overlooking an overgrown garden at one end and a tiny kitchen at the other. I saw a lot of Paul and Patsy and being together was like old times. We went on long walks through the woods or made music. One wall of my room was entirely covered with musical instruments I'd collected on my travels – Indian flutes, guitars, sitars, bongos, drums. On warm evenings we would take the instruments, big cushions and some hash onto the mansion roof and talk, play music and meditate under the stars.

After some months Christiana joined me in England and it was wonderful to see her again and to talk together about the new life we were planning in Canada. We flew to Niagara Falls, got the Greyhound Bus to Toronto and then set off on the three-day train journey through the Rocky Mountains towards Vancouver. In my rucksack I had 200 LSD tablets – not for us, I was only smoking a little hash now and then and Christiana rarely used any drugs. I hadn't been at all happy with the idea, but we were aware that sooner or later the money I had would run out so the plan was to sell the LSD for income while I was looking around for a job in Vancouver.

We looked at Vancouver with satisfaction. It was a great city, richly wooded and surrounded by lovely mountains. Our rented apartment in a wooden house was in an idyllic setting. But within weeks of our arriving there our dreams of a settled and happy future together began to seem unattainable.

To begin with, our confrontations with piles of paperwork and officials seemed unlikely to result in any possibility of us becoming accepted as immigrants. And the second major problem was that I just couldn't get a job. All the travelling we'd done in the two years we'd been together had eaten up most of my money. Even with the money from selling the LSD, things looked bad financially. I had no references, little real training in anything skilled and the vacancies were few and far between.

But by far the most distressing problem was that things were not working out between the two of us. The love and warmth were fading. We were growing apart now. Christiana had always been ambitious for her dancing career and the move to Vancouver had not given her the break she badly needed. She was determined to make a success of her career – but she was aware that time was not on her side. I began to feel guilty that I'd contributed to the problem, distracting her from dancing on top of all the problems and time-wasting she'd experienced when she was with Keith. Eventually she told me that she wanted to return to Marseilles – alone.

I had nowhere to go, except back to London – to think and rethink, to see what I could salvage of my life. I still had my yoga; it helped. But, in returning to the old scenes, I was aware of the fact that it was no longer the same for me. I was changing, and was more critical than ever of my old friends.

This criticism grew into a deeply felt frustration about what I judged to be the superficiality of most people's lives. Added to that was the burden of bitterness from the broken relationship with Christiana, which charged that frustration with anger and sad disillusionment. The faces I passed on the London streets seemed oblivious to reality, uncaring. I listened to their boring conversation and it grated on my ears. 'Nice day, isn't it!' Were they people or puppets? The lack of depth and sincerity hurt me. I felt suffocated in a society of pretenders.

I was at the crossroads again, it was obvious. My search for satisfaction, for meaning, for purpose, had taken me exploring an attractive side road. But it had turned out to be a dead end and my heart still pained from the disappointment. It was time to get back on the main road again.

I sought direction from the only source of inspiration open to me – the 'inner light' of yoga. This time there would be no turning back. The light pointed me again to the heart, the home of yoga – India. I was determined to try yet again to discover the simple lifestyle of the yogi mystics.

I sold everything except what I could cram into a leather pack I made myself. With my yoga carpet strapped to the underside of it, I said goodbye yet again to England – this time for good.

'Shoe shine, mister? Hashish? Good time?'

I brushed aside the chanting children at Bombay Airport and took the nearest taxi into the city. The cheap hotel the driver recommended was dirty, and there were fleas hopping around energetically on the wooden bed. But it did have a shower – and using it three or four times a day was the only thing that made life in that heavy humid climate bearable. Unfortunately, it was a shared room. The other occupant was a greasy-haired character with an evil sour face who spent most of his time flopped out on his bed fixing heroin.

I stayed in Bombay for about three weeks, immersing myself in the vibrant, colourful, crowded city life and travelling around the coastal area. Everywhere I went – along the lonely shore lined with tiny fishing boats, in the noisy markets thronged with herb stalls and snake charmers, in the cafés seeking refreshment from mint teas and cold drinks – I looked for significance. I looked for a sign, for direction, challenge, recognition. I looked for... I wasn't sure what. But somewhere, something had to make sense of me and for me. Or the loneliness and lack of purpose would drive me mad.

Everywhere I travelled I talked to people, asking questions. I asked them about the local gurus and their teachings. When the intensity of the heat and the exhaustion of the search defeated me I would take refuge in the little hotel to sit and meditate on my prayer mat. Sometimes I would think about Christiana, or Paul and Patsy. Or Dad. Once or twice I wrote letters to Dad, although I knew by now he never answered any of them. He'd definitely washed his hands of me.

I decided to get closer to the Himalayas – that seemed to be where all the mystic leaders congregated. I took the train to Delhi. The two-and-a-half-day journey was hot, dusty and slow – never more than twenty miles an hour. But it was a fascinating experience. The carriages of wooden benches were packed with Indian soldiers and people carrying chickens to market, the poor creatures hanging upside down, tied by their feet in bunches of three.

The journey was broken only by a brief conversation with a white man who arrived at some point and squeezed in next to me, ridiculously incongruous in a clean safari suit. He looked like an absent-minded professor from a second-rate comedy film. He started to talk to me, and I got interested when I realised he was saying something about God. But I couldn't make any sense of it. My attention kept wandering as I stared out of the window and watched the parrots and monkeys sitting chattering on the telegraph wires that stretched away to the horizon.

The man eventually gave up and left the carriage, pressing a little printed card into my hand. I read it, liked it and slipped it into my pocket. It was a little leaflet about the pearl; how it's formed and becomes perfect by the constant irritation of grains of sand. And it was about Jesus Christ. But I couldn't understand it. Although I would have liked to have talked more to the man in the suit he seemed to have disappeared.

From Delhi, where I stopped only briefly, I took a train a further day and a half journey to Rishikesh, a strange tantalising town at the mouth of the holy river – the Ganges – and in the foothills of the Himalayas. I found a tiny modern chalet to rent – there were a number dotted about on the lower slopes, and I was told they had been built for Mount Everest expeditions.

So here I continued my search. Wandering each day

by the river banks where the women scrubbed their washing on the huge sun-bleached boulders, I was continually amazed by the variety and strangeness of all I saw. Little groups of holy men or Tibetan monks would troop down to wash in the river, the droplets glistening on their smooth shaved heads. As they passed along in their saffron robes, the crowd would make way for them, and give them parcels of food.

All that I learnt of the Himalayas, a mixture of truth and legend, and of the holy men and gurus that lived there, both fascinated and frightened me. The 'inner light' of yoga told me that in the mountains I would find the teaching that my searching soul needed – and yet I was nervous of all the strange people I saw around me. After some weeks I decided to press on, across the Ganges.

The long motor boats that ferried people to and fro across the wide river mouth were worked by strangely attractive men who wore big gold earrings and brightly coloured turbans. Leaning over the side, I noticed the huge fish flashing grey in the water. These were the fish of the holy river and therefore could not be touched. Not only could they not be eaten, but I often saw the people – desperately poor themselves – feeding the fish from the banks.

On the other side I went up the marble steps from the boat and into a café that had trailing vines growing around low wooden beams. As I sipped my tea I became aware of the other customers. One man was dressed entirely in strips of seaweed. His strange dark beard was coiled like a spring and a string of beads dangled below his chin, suspended from one ear to the other. He held a trident in one hand.

Nearby a young white lad sat with his girlfriend. They muttered to each other in slurred French and I guessed from their confused state that they had been sitting there smoking hash for some time. At another table a young man sat alone, sombre, in a long white robe. A string round his neck was threaded with rupee notes.

I finished my tea and left, slinging my leather pack over my shoulder. Not far from the café was a miniature marble temple, with columns and tombstones decorated with weird paintings of mermaids and sea gods. Perfumed flower petals were strewn over the temple floor.

From there I walked on to the marketplace, where another even stranger sight startled me. A young boy – no more than seven or eight years old – was sitting in a deep trance on the top of a high stool, his arms outstretched stiffly in front of him. He wore just a brief loin cloth and his body was entirely painted a vivid pink all over except for two black circles round his staring eyes. His hair was thickly greased, standing up in a glossy point about two feet high. The sense of evil surrounding him was almost tangible and I felt I dared not look straight at the boy's eyes or somehow I would be lost. I discovered later that many such boys were used as 'diviners' for calling up evil spirits or visions.

Further along the road that wound between huge rocks, a small man was sitting cradling in his hands a brass goblet containing what I at first took to be blood. As he daubed a little of it on my forehead I realised it was the deep red dye or tilak used by Hindus. Beyond the man I glimpsed an entrance to a low building in the trees. From it came a regular pulsing beat of drums and cymbals.

Then I came to yet another small temple. Climbing the marble steps and passing between the dark grey stone pillars I saw a man in a long robe who bowed to me.

'Is there a guru here? Master? Yogi?' I asked.

He beckoned me to follow him up some steep steps onto the flat temple roof. He pointed to an old man with a long matted beard lying on a wooden bed and draped in a filthy rag.

The wrinkled face woke reluctantly.

'Ah, you one my disciples? From America? Bring money to guru? Good! Plenty money!' he said in harsh broken English.

With difficulty I explained that I was a student of yoga from England, seeking help.

It didn't take me long to realise that I was not in the presence of a wise teacher but of a con man trying to dupe anyone foolish enough to fall for it. I left, dispirited.

I continued on my journey, every day travelling a little deeper into the mountains. The higher I went, the stranger were the sights, the sounds and even the atmosphere. By night I lay awake under clear skies studded with bright diamond stars. The air was icy cold, sharp. By day it was hot, still, heavily scented with an intoxicating mixture of perfume, animal dung, incense and oil, spices and human exertion. I exchanged my jeans and embroidered shirts for looser, cooler white and saffron yellow Indian clothes. People I met now were often surprised to see a white man this far up on this side of the Ganges.

I took a few snapshots of some of the weirder sights

I encountered – like the tall thin man with yards and yards of black hair held in the shape of a pumpkin on his head who sat for hours motionless meditating, staring at a single leaf. Or the groups in a long grove of trees sitting like statues in the lotus position with little square hankies spread on the ground in front of them on which people placed money or food. A few of the photos came out – but many were inexplicably blank.

One of the ones that didn't come out is still imprinted in my memory. It was of an Indian I came across lying on a wooden bed at the edge of a mountain road overlooking the Ganges far below. He was dressed in a bizarre circus clown outfit of bright blue silk. His face was painted white, his staring eyes circled in black. And his dark hair was greased into the stiff high pointed style I'd seen before. His finger beckoned to me. I shuddered and walked on. A little further along the same road a group of dark aboriginal-looking men outside their rush huts were stewing something in a huge pot. They, too, beckoned me, but I shook my head and walked on, trying to look unconcerned.

I had now got to the point where to continue higher into the mountains would mean joining up with a group on ponies. Already I'd gone further than I should have done without an official permit. Permits were issued not only because of the sacredness of the mountains but apparently because there were gold deposits there.

What should I do? I was tired of searching and not finding. I was weary, too. And – I had to admit it – plain scared at times. I hesitated for several days, meditating on my mat, wanting to know what the yoga 'inner light' had to tell me. I listened hard – and then put my few belongings into my leather travelling pack. With a heavy heart, I turned my back on the higher slopes and ridges and set off back down the mountainside.

I wasn't altogether convinced about returning. And that was probably why the journey down was marked by detours and diversions. I was still waiting for the something dramatic that would make everything clear to me. I was persuaded by a persistent tourist to visit a commune of Krishna worshippers. I spent several days travelling to the commune, a huge house in an obscure place guarded by tall wrought iron gates. I arrived at nightfall, following the darting fireflies along the hedge-lined path to the entrance in the gathering gloom. I stayed just a few hours. As I watched those placid faces chanting 'Hare, hare Krishna' at a painted god on a wall, accompanied by the metallic jingle of their little cymbals, I felt I was no more than a spectator. I desperately wanted to belong. But this wasn't for me. As I saw the first signs of the sun rising over the distant mountains, I picked up my leather pack and left.

Another diversion was a two-week intensive course in Buddhism I was persuaded to endure. Along with about thirty other people I sat for hours in a large hall trying to empty my mind and cleanse it with the Buddhist philosophy. Near the end of the fortnight I asked for an audience with the Burmese leader to talk about some of his teachings. As I started to pour out my own feelings he began to laugh. He laughed loud and long, the sound stabbing deep into me. That was really the last straw, all I could take. Within a day or two I boarded a plane. First stop – Marseilles.

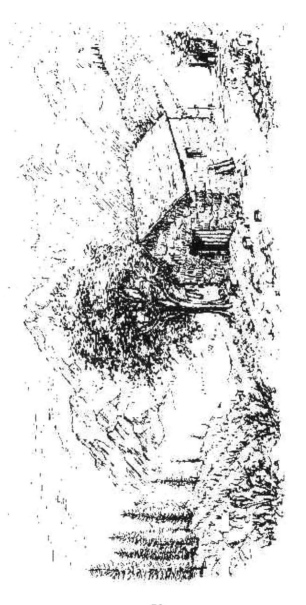

CHAPTER 5

The stopover at Marseilles was little more than a half-hearted attempt to rediscover something good, something lost. But Christiana was cold and impatient with me, even a little embarrassed to see me as I stood on her doorstep in my dusty saffron trousers and top. She had no time for me now, that was plain. She told me she was into a different kind of yoga – Tibetan. By hard work she was beginning to re-establish her career as a dancer, and there would be no distractions this time. I said goodbye as graciously as I could and took the next plane to London.

Was I giving up my search? True, there was a sense of despair hanging heavy on my shoulders as I went back to my home country – the place I'd so determinedly left nearly a year previously, thinking I'd never return. But greater than the sense of defeat was the sense of relief. All that I'd been striving for seemed inaccessible – too hard, too far, too evil. I was weary of travelling and exhausted by my repeated failure to meet people who were sincere, who understood what I was longing for. The future was blank, uninviting. But I hadn't abandoned yoga. Those who practiced it might have let me down. They surely had. But I clung hard to the theory, the philosophy of yoga. Indeed it seemed all I had left. I wanted to train my body and mind to live a life of the spirit, unconcerned with the material.

Back in Surbiton, I was strangely glad to find Paul and Patsy welcoming, and within a few days I moved into a little bedsit close to their flat. But the time had not yet come when I was ready to settle down. Incredibly, after just six months I was making plans for yet another excursion abroad!

This time, though, there were very different motives for travelling. The initiative came from Paul and Patsy. They said they'd like to go to Morocco to see a different way of life and to get some hash to sell in England. Over the years they'd been the only consistent friends I'd had and I didn't want to lose them now. They'd never been abroad and, perhaps rather patronisingly, I felt they needed me along to keep an eye on them. Paul was not a tolerant person. He was serious, intense and had no real sense of humour. I had real fears about how he'd cope with the very different mentality he'd find in North Africa. I talked to them both about the cultural and personality differences I'd found abroad, but I was doubtful that they'd really taken it in.

Eventually we hit upon a plan I was happy with. I would go on ahead and spend a few weeks searching out a nice house in the mountains and then send for Paul and Patsy to join me. They saw me off at Gatwick Airport a few weeks later as I flew off on the first stage of the journey, to Gibraltar. From there I took a boat to Tangier, and then hitchhiked to Tetuan.

Tetuan was a lovely town. Old whitewashed houses stood among the cypress, almond, orange and eucalyptus trees. For the first time I saw the gaily dressed Rif peasant women I was to find working in the fields all over the region. They wore full red, white and blue striped skirts and wide straw hats with pompoms bobbing from the brim. Leather gaiters tied with thongs protected their legs from the thorny bushes.

From Tetuan a packed bus took me to Chechaquen, another fresh, sunny town with cobbled streets and blue and white houses nestling at the foot of the Rif mountains. It had an almost continental air about it. People chatted at tables outside cafés scattered along the tree-lined avenues. There were bustling markets selling fruit, woven materials, crude pots and fascinating musical instruments.

I pressed on towards the heart of the country. After a few nights in Chechaquen I went on to the large town of Fez, which remains in my memory as the place where I was soundly cheated by a small boy. He promised – in return for money, of course – to lead me through the medina, the huge sprawling market that was literally a maze to all but the local people. My young guide slipped away when my back was turned, leaving me stranded. It took me almost the whole day to find my way out, wandering among the stalls of trays, pottery and incense looking hopelessly for recognisable landmarks among the countless stone arches and identical little alleyways.

Not far from Fez, I arrived at a delightful village in the Atlas Mountains where I thought it likely I could find a home for Paul, Patsy and myself. On one side of the village on the hillside I discovered an estate of white flat-roofed houses with big sloping gardens. At the bottom of each garden open latrines flowed down into a muddy stream which ran right through the village. I set out to find out if any of the houses were empty.

The tough Berber people who lived in the village were quite excited to see me. Apart from the odd student who would arrive and hang about the coffee bar for a few days before moving on, Westerners did not come here very often. Talking to them I found out that the estate I had seen was for widows and their children. The widows, I soon noticed, were all marked by a cross tattooed on their cheek, nose or forehead.

I was directed to Omar, who appeared to be a kind of headman in the village. He was a dark, kind-faced man with dazzling white teeth. He lived in relative luxury in a large flat with his wife, a whole horde of children, and his parents-in-law. Magnanimously, he invited me to eat with the family – and I was obviously an honoured guest as the best silverware was carefully produced for the table.

Omar knew a little English and we managed to communicate fairly well with an odd mix of phrases and hand signals. By the end of the evening he was aware that I'd like to stay in the village and needed accommodation. By the next day he'd negotiated something for me; I was given a concrete cellar in one of the white houses in the estate, owned by a widow and three or four giggling adolescent daughters. Amid much curiosity, I settled myself into the cellar, unpacking my large leather bag. The room itself was the barest of shelters, containing just a blanket and a rug and no furniture at all. There were no windows, either, just a huge heavy wooden door. It was freezing there at night.

Despite the accommodation, I liked the village and the Berber people were generous and hospitable, although they stared at me openly and without embarrassment everywhere I went. After a few days I wrote giving directions for Paul and Patsy to join me. I hoped that within a matter of months I would be able to rent a whole house in the village for the three of us.

The passing weeks did not make me less of a local curiosity! As I walked in the village, the Berbers would stop and stare, smile, grin, even try to engage me in stilted conversation. Each morning I would go up onto the flat roof of the house where I was staying, spread out my prayer mat and sit down for a time of meditation. But often I was acutely aware of the puzzled looks and even laughter from the neighbouring rooftops, where the women would pause from hanging out their washing in the bright sun to watch me.

I was quickly befriended by an original character called Sealli. He was a Moroccan who lived with his coal-black wife and their daughter in a house on the next block. Sealli was one of the Sherif or 'noble people' of the area. He dressed proudly in what he felt was Western style – Western trousers tucked into big black wellingtons, a shirt with rolled sleeves, and a penknife stuck through his leather belt. His wife used to be a cleaner at the embassy – a fact no one was allowed to forget as she always wore white sheets wrapped round her ample body with the words AMERICAN EMBASSY boldly printed at the corners!

Soon after we got to know each other, Sealli grabbed me by the hand one evening and virtually dragged me round to his house, insisting I was to share a meal with him and his family.

The main room in the concrete house was totally bare apart from a red line painted halfway up the white walls. Beyond that was the bedroom – a tiny square room with a concrete ledge on all four walls with cushions on it, which served as the bed for everyone.

Sealli worked in the local slaughterhouse, I discovered. And that was the reason why we dined that evening on a huge dish of lamb fried with whole peppers and sliced aubergines. It also turned out that Sealli was keen for himself and his wife and child to learn English – and he was determined that I should not only become their teacher but their permanent guest. Within a few days I gave in to his persistent persuasion and moved into the cramped little concrete home.

I had not yet heard from Paul and Patsy so I wrote again. All in all, apart from a certain loneliness, the weeks passed pleasantly enough. I spent hours wandering in the markets, watching the stallholders prepare the local delicacy – snails collected from under the rocks on the mountains and boiled. In the medina there was always something of interest to see such as snake charmers attracting the crowds with their strange musical instruments – huge tambourine-like instruments with two vibrating strings lying against the skin. There were wandering beggars prepared to sink needles into their arms and legs to get people to throw them money.

I drank tea in the sultry chi houses. Or I wandered on the peaceful hillsides, often stopping to chat with the groups of sombre old men who were always there knitting little circular hats or making bamboo flutes for sale. I took to wearing the gelaba – the long-sleeved full-length hooded striped robe that was commonly worn there, and that way avoided some of the staring and questioning.

I was content for the time being to continue to live with the entertaining Sealli and his family. The efforts he made to impress me were so amusing, especially his keen attempts to show me how dedicated he was to the Muslim faith. He made a great show of his five-times-daily prayer ritual! Sometimes, though, our friendship was sorely tested, like the occasion I was forced to endure the strange ceremonies of some religious custom that in my mind resembled the Jewish Passover. With due solemnity a ram was killed and, according to custom, the household had to spend the first evening of the festival eating all the inner organs of the animal, stewed in a sort of gravy. The gruesome sight and the rank smell of the animal lungs bobbing about in the deep brown tureen repulsed me. But Sealli was firm. And somehow I got through it!

As the weeks turned to months I was more and more worried. Why hadn't Paul and Patsy arrived? I had heard nothing from England. I was running seriously short of money. Even with Sealli's generous hospitality I was reduced to my last few pounds. And, whether it was the climate or the unusual diet or the increasing anxiety, I now had real reason to be concerned about my health. My body was plagued with a strange weakness, a lethargy I couldn't shake off. The nights were extremely cold and I spent more and more of them in bouts of shivering and feverishness beneath my thin blanket.

Sometimes, to give my aching body a little relief, I would spend a few of my remaining coins on a visit to the village sauna pool for a hot bath. This was a primitive place, though, and it took some courage to go there. On the edge of the village at the base of a muddy hill was a low concrete building. After taking your outer clothes off, the procedure was to go down a dark tunnel into a sort of cave divided into three rooms, all ankle-deep in muddy water. In the corner of the cave was a hole from which bubbled hot water. Bathers were issued with a wooden bucket with which to collect the steamy water to wash in. One day at the pool a native masseur took pity on me and put me through a terrifying ordeal of strenuous exercises and massage. He literally held me powerless on top of him while he stretched my arms and legs in every direction. Leaving the cave, I felt a totally different person, my legs like jelly as I walked along the streets.

My illness made me feel weak and nervous, and matters became worse when a young North African heroin addict came to live nearby and began to terrorise me. He sensed how vulnerable I was and seemed to take pleasure from constantly harassing and threatening me, and twice he sneaked into Sealli's home and stole things from my bag.

I began to despair of Paul and Patsy ever coming. It was now about ten weeks since I'd first written to tell them to come and join me, and I'd written other letters since, appealing to them to come as soon as possible.

Practically penniless, I rummaged through my leather pack looking for something to sell. Nothing of any value left. But then my eyes rested on the heavy gold ring I wore. It had an unusual design of a gypsy stamped onto it. It's no exaggeration to say it must have weighed an ounce. I'd bought it in Canada for £100, but I was certain it was worth a lot more. Asking around, it seemed that the best place to sell the ring was at the big port of Casablanca. Leaving messages everywhere for Paul and Patsy, I set off – on a journey that was to prove a nightmare.

I hitchhiked to Meknes, a quiet market town with beautiful orange groves, and then on to Rabat. Rabat was a strange place. There was a large graveyard on the beach and at high tide the waves came right up over the tombstones. I quite often roughed it by sleeping out at night on a beach – but here I couldn't face lying down among the dead! Some local children playing nearby showed me an abandoned railway carriage and I climbed in there for a restless night. At first light I was off along the coast road again. By now my small supplies of food had run out, so had my money, and I felt that I was getting weaker and weaker.

People I passed stared at me. Hardly surprising, I suppose. By now I looked and smelt like a tramp and was too ill to care. My clothes were dusty and dishevelled. The bright sea and sky hurt my eyes. By the roadside I spotted some juicy purple cacti-like plants, and I crammed handfuls of them greedily into my mouth, little bothered about the consequences although I had already been warned that these local fruits, though delicious, caused dreadful skin irritations which lasted for days. I sat down and swallowed enough to satisfy my hunger. How wretched I felt, how totally desolate!

The pains in my stomach eased a little. But I was conscious of a deeper and more desperate hunger that remained untouched. 'God... if you are... if you care... can't you see the need I'm in?' But how could God help me? Was I expecting some kind of divine rescue mission to come hurtling out of the dazzling blue sky? With an effort I pulled myself on to my feet and walked on, pinning all my hopes on something a bit more real than God – that little piece of gold on my finger.

Towards the end of that afternoon a young guy sitting at a roadside café beckoned to me and offered me a share of his food – a kind of doughy sugarless bun, quite horrible to taste, but I ate it ravenously. He said he was going to visit relatives in Casablanca and we agreed to travel on together. At dusk we reached the place where his relatives lived and parted. I set off again into the night, hitching a lift in a Volkswagen van along the main road into the town.

I hated Casablanca. Mainly because of the bitter disappointment of discovering that after the exhausting journey I could only get £10 for my ring. I searched the city asking for a better price. But it appeared that the local gold was darker and considered better than Canadian gold. I stayed two nights at a youth hostel and took the bus south to Marrakesh. I'd decided that the only hope of raising some money was to buy some hash with the money from the ring and trade that.

Marrakesh was quite different. The fresh mountain air was exhilarating and I began to feel a bit better. But I wasn't able to buy any hash. So it was another bus journey, this time to Fez. Here I met an addict I'd seen around before and he told me of a small village in the mountains where there were several farms where I could get what I was looking for.

The 'grass' grew abundantly on the farms, in shrubs four or five feet high in steps cut into the steep mountain slopes. The pollen from the plants was used to make solid blocks of hash. The farmers here also grew gourds and other vegetables.

So here I stayed for several weeks, sharing a bare cottage on a cliff with several other Western hippies in Ketama on the same errand. We all slept by night under a huge bug-ridden carpet beneath the walnut trees, and by day we wandered on the hillsides and haggled over prices with the hash farmers.

While I was there I witnessed a local wedding procession – an experience not to be forgotten. A procession of people in long snow-white robes and mitred headdresses marched through the little farm settlement blowing strange screeching pipes. At the head of the parade was a bronzed young man wearing an animal skin, beating a small drum. The procession marched around the area playing on their disturbing pipes for two days! A week later I visited another farm in the valley below, only to hear the same screeching and witness the same wedding procession still in full swing!

Although hash was grown so openly in this remote area, trying to smuggle it out somewhere else was not an easy proposition. This time I was not able to get hold of anything as sophisticated as a corset or a false-bottomed suitcase. I had to be content with hiding bags of hash inside my trousers! I boarded one of the few buses which passed through the region and held my breath when police got on at a village stop some miles further on. They ordered one young guy off the bus with a gun in his back, to be searched – and then with relief I saw them wave the bus on – detaining the hippy for a thorough ransack of all his bags.

The danger wasn't quite over, though. The sullen-looking ticket inspector slowly working his way down the bus stopped at me and fixed me with a menacing squint. Inspecting my ticket, he hissed into my ear, 'You, boy. You carry plenty hash, good stuff? Pay money or you meet police next stop, see?'

It wouldn't do to respond to his threats. At first I pretended not to know what he was talking about. As he got more persistent I tried to convince him I was a sick man, clutching my stomach and swaying a little in my seat. I needed fresh air, I said, and moved into an empty seat nearer the door at the back. At the next stop the inspector was talking to someone at the front of the bus, so I seized my chance. Just as the bus was about to jolt off again, I dived off, sprinted a few yards into a narrow ditch and jumped in. Crouching low, I waited breathlessly until the grumbling engine sounds had died away.

Looking around, I saw I was on a wide dusty plain, broken only by a few dry bushes and huge grey boulders. I ran on, up into the hills and into a little village. Ahead I could see the road, little more than a cart track, which I knew I must keep in sight or be hopelessly lost. I paid some local children to show me part of the way over a treacherous, rocky, fast-flowing river. Later I saw a man on horseback who I feared was a policeman, so I hid in a heather field until he had passed. Then some hours later I saw a white Renault coming up the road behind me. Police? Drug smugglers? By now I was too exhausted to care, and decided to risk hitching a lift. The car slowed and inside sat three prosperous-looking businessmen. No doubt they were big-time smugglers, but I didn't ask any questions, just sat tight.

Finally, I got back to Fez. I spent the next few weeks

selling my hash, mainly to tourists, some to soldiers at a nearby camp. Still there was no sign of Paul and Patsy.

The days that followed became a blur. In my misery and loneliness I took to smoking lots of hash again I submerged myself in the hippy hash party scene, spending most of my time semi-coherent, playing my drums and bongos for hours. Drug taking, together with lack of proper food, sleep and shelter began to take a heavy toll on my weakened body.

One night I nearly died through my own carelessness. The only heating I had was an old metal bucket pierced with holes in which I burned olive wood. The local people warned me not to take it indoors as the fumes were dangerous. But one night, desperately cold, I took the bucket into my little windowless room. Within an hour or so I was only partly conscious and felt I was going mad. I began to scream and bang my head against the wall, so intense were the pains in my skull. Fortunately, the villagers heard my cries of torment and came rushing in. 'Nathac, nathac!' they shouted to each other, and dragged me out into the cold night air. They rubbed oil into my head and tied it round with huge, shiny, flat green leaves, holding me down as I writhed in agony.

Thankfully, my old friend Omar took pity on me and took me in a state of near collapse into his house again. For two weeks I lay tossing under a thin blanket on a wooden bed in his house. At times I was feverishly hot, at others I shivered with cold and my body was wracked with cramps. I was blinded by strange stabbing pains in my eyes that almost drove me insane. I had no medicines of any kind. Sometimes I tried to put salt into my eyes in the hope that whatever was infecting them would be cleansed by it. Never before, not in any London gutter or blank-walled prison cell had I felt so totally godforsaken. All kinds of strange illusions tormented me, frighteningly vivid, nightmarish. The past was a dream, the future unwanted. All that was real was the hurt of each minute. I ceased caring that it could or would ever be any different.

Then one day the vision dancing in my mind was not threatening. It was familiar. It was a vision of Paul and Patsy. Paul and Patsy travelling. To me? Yes, of course, they were coming to me at last! I fell back on to the bed and slept deeply.

The next morning, shivering and drained, I awoke early. Raising myself up stiffly on the bed I propped my back against the cold wall, pulled my legs up and gathered my pathetic blanket around me as best I could. I tried to clear my mind to meditate.

After a few minuets I felt a hand on my shoulder.

'Terry, we're here!'

The warmth from Patsy's hand penetrated the blanket. But I didn't dare open my eyes. Paul shook my arm.

'Hey, man we're here!'

I should have been happy. But the long wait of half a year had made my heart hard against them, And my soul had forgotten how to be glad.

CHAPTER 6

Only slowly as I emerged from that strange distant world of sickness could I feel able to communicate with Paul and Patsy again. They stayed with me, sharing the small room at the home of the obliging Omar, although some of his family were far from happy about the arrangement.

I wondered, though, if things could ever be the same for the three of us. Paul, in particular, seemed tense and moody. He didn't get on with the local people and it irritated me that he made so little effort. Most days we spent wandering around the bazaars or the olive farms near the town. People everywhere were welcoming, inviting. In the markets they would grab us by the sleeves and look hopeful if we took an interest in what was on their stalls. On the farms we would be encouraged to drink tea and smoke. Sometimes people would invite me into their homes. I felt embarrassed to discover they thought I was some kind of travelling wise man or fakir. Looking at the weird way I dressed, it was easy to see why. Everything I wore had great significance for me. My thick padded tasselled Afghani waistcoat was embroidered in three colours – green to represent the earth, blue for the sky and red for fire. Shapes of the moon and sun were cut out of my high leather boots. I wore a brown flowerpot-shaped hat and a faded green t-shirt. Around one arm I had a highly glossed clay bangle from a Pakistani temple, decorated in shades of green, red and black, which was supposed to be of great religious significance. I also wore an earring which was a round coin-shaped piece of mother of pearl. And my two companions dressed in a style which was no less outlandish.

We spent a lot of time immersed in making our own music – playing bongos, clay drums and wooden pipes. We made several instruments of our own, experimenting with things we found around us – nails, pieces of cotton and old bits of wood. And there was always my yoga and meditation.

Paul soon wanted to move out of the town into the seclusion of the hills. It wasn't just that he wanted to be away from the bustle of the town. He said he suspected that Omar's mother, an old woman who did a lot of cooking for the family, was trying to poison us. It seemed a fantastic idea at first, but it was true that all three of us had bouts of illness. Certainly the tolerance the old woman had shown towards me in the past had disappeared now that there were two extra mouths to feed. And the relationship between me and Omar's wife was increasingly strained, too. Following my recovery from illness she'd been hanging around me a lot, giving me furtive glances, or strange little smiles. Because of my close friendship with Omar – who remained totally oblivious to both his mother's antagonism and his wife's not always discreet attempts to impress me – I did my best to keep my distance from both women.

One day the opportunity to move out came about through a chance meeting in Fez market with a well-off French Moroccan and his girlfriend. They spoke a little English and told us they worked in the theatre and films – and their glamorous lifestyle certainly backed up this claim. They took us to their home – a large white-walled house surrounded by orange trees. Sitting on their verandah sipping cool drinks, they pointed to a small settlement of red-roofed houses in the distance.

'We've got a little house there, in the hills beyond that village,' said the man, extravagantly. 'Would you three like to stay there for a while?'

We went back to Omar's to talk it over. Paul and Patsy were keen to go, but I didn't want to offend Omar. I remembered how he'd stayed with me when I'd been so ill. His loyalty was touching; in contrast I still felt that Paul and Patsy had let me down badly by coming to join me so late. Should I let them go their own way and stay where I was?

Early next morning I went up on to the roof quietly, hoping to have a time there alone to meditate on the decision. But as I climbed the steps softly I realised that the old mother and one of her cronies from the town were up there together. They had some bunches of herbs drying in the sun, and they were busy with a big bowl and a pestle. As I watched, unseen by them, they added a large multicoloured beetle to the mixture in the bowl and carried on grinding, muttering like a couple of witches over a brew in a cauldron. I didn't know if it was poisonous or not – but the scene had been enough to convince me I didn't want to stay long enough to find out!

We went back to see our actor friend about renting his cottage. Now he seemed to regret his earlier generous offer. It turned out that the cottage wasn't really his, but his father's.

'My father's a very strict man. I'm not sure he'd be happy. I should really have talked it over with him, but he's away on business at the present.'

He bit his top lip nervously.

'Look,' said Patsy. 'We promise we'll take good care of the place. A good rent for you. A great place for us to stay in. Your father need never know. You say he's away most of the time, anyway.'

Finally, still hesitating, he gave in to us, handed over a bunch of keys and sketched out the route to the cottage.

Omar was upset when I broke the news that we were leaving. But, magnanimous to the last, he agreed to take us and our few bits of luggage on to our next address in his battered old car. I begged him to come and visit us whenever he could. I knew I was really going to miss him.

It was a lovely cottage in a beautiful setting and I felt good just being there, away from the heat and crowds of Fez. Here I knew I could finish with hash once and for all and concentrate on my meditation. I felt I was really progressing to deeper things, tapping inner resources in a new way. I had visions of setting up my own meditation class in time. I talked it over with Paul and Patsy as we went on long frequent walks along the sheep tracks in the hills, gathering the dried cones we used to make fires in the evenings.

The peace I experienced here was short lived. One night, after just a few weeks, we were awakened by a thunderous knocking on the front door. It was a party of four local policemen, accompanied by the young French Moroccan actor. What followed was a very confusing scene which almost ended with us being removed to the police station! Neither the actor nor anyone else would speak any English to us, but we realised that we were being accused of trespassing, and worked out that our friend had got cold feet about us staying here. Perhaps the father he was so scared of was coming home. Whatever it was, our explanations to the police fell on deaf or uncomprehending ears. I tried to ask for Omar to come and help us explain things. I went down to the village square and tried to phone him, but could get no reply.

So we had no choice but to pack up and leave the cottage. We headed further up into the hills. Paul was keen to visit the hash plantations there that I'd previously visited and I could think of no real objection, though by now I was more than a little disillusioned with travelling around.

There was no room for us to stay in the little settlement I'd camped at before, but we were directed further up a winding mountain track and into a wood. As evening came on and the temperature began to fall, we finally arrived, very tired, at a wide clearing surrounded by tall firs. A roughly built cottage stood in the clearing and to one side of it an odd wooden construction that looked like a large loft raised about six feet off the ground on stilts. A clear pebbled stream ran past both buildings and disappeared into the thick wood beyond.

I took an immediate dislike to the middle-aged man with a tough scheming face who answered our knock on the cottage door. Still, we were desperate for somewhere to sleep. He showed us up the steps into the odd shack on stilts. The long low-ceilinged building was divided into several rooms, with a cooking area at one end and at the other about half a dozen small bare wooden beds. I lay down gratefully, cold and sweating, realising that my body was not yet fully recovered from my long illness. I longed for some proper blankets but had nothing. We were quite high above the snow line here and the air really took my breath away. It was exhilarating – but so cold at night.

Some time in the middle of that night the other residents of this strange 'farm' arrived home: four young Moroccan men, who were relatives of the man in charge. All were in boisterous high spirits.

The next morning we introduced ourselves. They were traders with a regular business passing hash to big dealers in Tangier. They showed us the flashing police light they carried and pointed us over to the trees where they had a white Renault hidden – their passport through the border on their many drug runs. They were proud of their success in crime and delighted in telling us in great detail all about their various escapades.

Our plan, as far as we had one, was to stay here just long enough for Paul and Patsy to buy some top quality hash from one of the local farmers. I was just not interested. I spent a depressing few weeks in the wooded clearing with little money and even less food, while Paul was out haggling over prices. Our miserable farmer fed us on fried pigeons' eggs and hunks of bread. Most days I sat alone by the stream; sometimes Patsy would join me and we'd play some music, but it seemed to come out rather melancholy.

When Paul completed his deal I wanted to leave immediately and suggested going somewhere near the sea. After a lot of trouble we managed to get a rare coach going to the coast near Al Hoceima. The coach ride was the kind of alarming trip we were getting accustomed to – erratic speeds, rough roads, and impossible hairpin bends. Coming down from the mauve and green hillsides where the gaily dressed Rif peasant women were gathering herbs, we saw the cobbled streets of a seaside town. Getting off the coach we could see it was a pretty place, the main street lined with trees, the houses neat and tidy. But the town didn't have a lot of spirit to it; it was strangely quiet. The few people that were out in the streets seemed mute, going their way mildly, automatically. They looked as if they were under a spell.

At the town's only hotel the tanned manager in the spotless black hooded gelaba shook his head, eyeing our shabby clothes intently. I felt he could even see how much – or rather, how little – money we had in our pockets. No room, he said.

We argued. But he was firm. We went off to the nearest chi house to consider the next step as we drank black minted tea. The place was full of old men smoking kif pipes and watching a film on a decrepit TV in the corner.

Chilly evening was approaching and we knew we had only one choice – to throw ourselves on the mercy of the fastidious hotel manager. He knew that, too. Finally, he agreed to take us in – if we'd pay double the going rate for a room. And in advance, of course.

Sitting alone by the sea the next day was a good place to meditate. I had to face up to the fact that my relationship with Paul and Patsy was disintegrating. In the past our friendship had been strengthened by the unity of minds moving in the same direction. But not any more. I'd tried to forgive them for all those months of hardship I'd suffered waiting for them, although in my mind they'd never been able to offer any adequate explanation. Paul was so casual he'd hardly bothered to try to excuse himself. 'We had a bit of hassle getting the bread together, man.' He had no understanding of what I'd been through at all.

But more than that, our roads seemed to be diverging. I was beginning to put drugs and dealing behind me. They both still needed to take drugs. The urgency inside me to find out answers to questions that had been with me for years was not only still there but growing. That Paul and Patsy did not seem to share this was a disappointment I was coming to terms with. In the past our friendship had been vital to my wellbeing. Now I felt more self-contained. My recent experiences had not only taught me independence but taught me to prefer it to social reliance. True, I often felt lonely. But now I wanted to go it alone. I still liked Paul and Patsy immensely, but the love and need had gone. My very personal search for meaning in life, for purpose, had become of supreme importance to me – more important, I realised, than they were.

I walked along the coast kicking at the sand and shingle. A little fishing boat was just landing in one of the coves and for a few coins I bought some fresh herrings and sprats for our supper.

I took a different route back to the hotel that led past fascinating old temple ruins and a cemetery on a hilltop. What was left of the temple's protecting wall ran right along the edge of a sheer cliff, the sea pounding in a small inlet far below. I climbed down. Some of the smooth, wave-polished pebbles were enormous – a foot or so across. Some were arranged in fantastic and unnatural heaps, balanced one on another. Round the point I glimpsed what looked like an old lighthouse and close by an expensive-looking motorboat that seemed out of place. The whole scene made me think of smuggling and shipwrecks; it was mysterious and suspicious.

It was a desolate place, too. Apart from the fisherman, I'd seen just three other people that whole day – two Rif girls who passed carrying huge packs of straw strapped to their backs and reaching several feet above their heads, and a shepherd boy out with his scrawny flock. He eyed me suspiciously and kept his distance.

But the next morning the sleepy town was transformed. It was market day. Hundreds of people streamed down from the hills carrying baskets of dates, herbs and hand-woven clothes. The stench of their horses and mud-caked mules filled the streets.

Inevitably, I couldn't reach much agreement with Paul and Patsy over where to go next. Paul wanted to see more of Morocco. I'd had enough. But I wanted to avoid an argument, so I agreed to travel with them on the next coach to Ketama and then on to Chechowen. And it was there that something unusual precipitated our parting.

We arrived there at the start of the feast of Ramadan, which meant that we could buy no food between sunrise and sunset. We were sitting at a pavement café at the unearthly hour of three o'clock in the morning when a Moroccan man appeared from nowhere and launched into an address aimed at me.

'I know who you are. And I know where you have

come from. You must stay here in this town until I come back to you. In two weeks. I have business away for two weeks. Then I come for you. You will live with me.'

The man smiled and then disappeared just as suddenly as he had appeared. I should have laughed off the whole silly incident, but I couldn't. The affair had frightened me, although I couldn't really say why. He had spoken to me as if he'd known me and it felt evil.

Suddenly I was sickened by this whole way of life; sick and tired of being short of money, short of food, short of confidence, tired of feeling ill. I was overwhelmed with a deep depression and decided immediately to return home to England. I felt very vulnerable, out of control. I needed the safe ground of home.

Paul and Patsy announced that they would press on to Marrakesh, and we parted without regret. I had enough money for a ticket to Tangier and I persuaded them to give me a small packet of dope to sell there. It wasn't quite enough to finance the rest of my trip home, but four hippies I knew from the drug farms in the hills gave me a bit more dope to sell and finally I'd got together just about enough.

I bought my plane ticket to Madrid and went to a café to while away the last few hours before take-off. Two English boys came up and started chatting to me. They could see how low I was feeling and seemed to want to cheer me up. They looked incongruous, with neat clothes and short haircuts. They were travelling around on an old-fashioned motorbike.

'You need to go up to the hospital and get yourself

fixed up,' said one, looking at me in a concerned way that made me feel warm inside.

'Yes,' said his friend. 'There are some really great Jesus people up there. They'll help you for sure.'

After they'd gone I stared at my empty cup, thinking. Jesus. Who was he anyway? Just another prophet? But those boys were right about me needing help.

Full of indecision, I left the café and asked someone the way to the hospital. I must have taken a wrong turning or something, because I wandered around for ages and couldn't find it. Another dead end. I must get home, I thought. I must get home.

I just made it to the plane. From Madrid I got a train through France and eventually got to Calais and on a boat to Southampton.

Back in Kingston, I gratefully submerged myself in the old crowd. In their own way they were glad to have me back. My body slowly responded to an easier life and I began to feel fitter again. My mind, though, was not so easily healed. Failure and frustration were strong feelings that often swamped me. I was so hurt that in all my travelling, all my searching, I really hadn't found the peace of mind, the satisfaction that I wanted. There were still so many questions unanswered. The need to know the why, the how, the when, the what, the purpose to my very existence, was still there. Occasionally, fed with excitement, the hunger was briefly satisfied. But only for a while.

CHAPTER 7

Over the months that followed I returned to my slot within Kingston's hippy subculture, giving me security of a sort. I moved into a commune with about thirty others, mainly students. It was the end of the 1960s and young people were revolutionaries. The talk was of the latest Pink Floyd record, the meaning of truth, free love and what it meant to be totally honest. We philosophised over the creation of the universe and wondered about the goodness in nature. We went into the woods, lit fires and sat round and talked some more. We carried sunflower seeds around in little pouches and dropped them into people's gardens.

Yes, now I see how naive it all was! But then we believed sincerely that we were making a real contribution to a world-changing revolution. One night we filled the whole flat with hundreds of balloons. We were always thinking of crazier and crazier things to do, to experiment with. We were looking for ultimate pleasure-giving experiences and felt heady with sensations of power.

The drugs we smoked daily distorted our reason and made sense of nonsense, I see that now. Yes – I'd gone back to smoking hash. It all helped to make me part of the crowd. But when I looked in the mirror I saw a wrinkled aged face that shocked me and I felt physically bowed over and knew I walked these days with a stoop.

I was at the centre of it all, committed to the commune. Or was I? Try as I might, I couldn't help but see that there was beginning to be a gulf between me and the rest. I was apparently involved but there was a curious distance, a detachment I couldn't deny. Sometimes I found myself staring at the rest of them as if I was a spectator watching a play.

To begin with I had enjoyed an exalted position in the group as undisputed resident source of knowledge on things Eastern and religious. People came to listen to my expansive accounts of my travels. I was looked to for advice on meditation, on yoga practices.

As time passed – and I realise now this was largely the influence of the hash I was smoking – I began to suffer increasingly from intense paranoia. I began to imagine that everyone who laughed was laughing at me, that friends engaged in private conversations must be talking about me – gossiping, criticising, plotting. The bodies, the choking atmosphere, the stench of the flea-ridden cats, the nauseating piles of unwashed crockery littering the kitchen – all of this pushed me into black moods when all I could think about was to plan my own death. I'd tried before to commit suicide by overdosing and thought often of cutting my wrists or jumping in front of a train.

I was increasingly disillusioned with people. I thought a lot about Paul and Patsy and felt they'd betrayed me. I thought a lot about my family, too, and that hurt. On my last trip abroad I'd left everything I owned in the care of my younger brother, Phil. I'd come back to find he and his friends had helped themselves to all my possessions, using some, selling others.

When Paul and Patsy did return to London a few months after I did, I made some attempt to repair the damaged, numbed relationship. I confronted them one day and poured out my feelings in a way I hadn't been able to before.

'Six years we've been close, sharing, living together. But you always seem to let me down. I can't feel I trust you any more. You don't seem to feel the way I do.'

They shrugged and turned away. I was disturbed, disillusioned.

'I want to tell you both something. I believe that in less than three months I'm going to be with God.'

What was I saying? The words had just come out, but surely they weren't mine? I was at the end of the road. Yet somehow I felt I was closer to God.

It was out of disgust for human relationships, the rejection, the wounding inside, that I turned more and more away from people and into myself. People were parasites. They came to me for drugs, for what they could get from me. Not for any value they saw in me as a fellow human being.

I moved out of the commune and into a bedsit. As well as my longing to get away from the group, there was the constant harassment of police raids now. More and more I shut myself away, alone with my questions. If there was no love, no peace in being with other people because of all their failings, what about God? Was there a God who could be found who would make sense of it all? If there was no God then I was convinced that death was preferable to all this loneliness and degradation.

I went for long walks in the woods and parks,

imagining that if I meditated long enough, deep enough, I would get through to God. And I read avidly, mostly books on the occult and spiritualism, searching like a prospector with gold fever.

One summer evening I'd been persuaded to go out with the whole gang. They decided to go off to a pub in Surbiton. As we strolled along the road I was there in the middle of them all, my face looking interested, talking and smiling. Inside I felt desperate to get away from them. My mind was in turmoil and my heart felt like a lead weight.

At the bottom of the road we neared a church. It loomed solid out of the gloomy dusk. I could make out the figure of Christ on a huge stained-glass window. For a second or two my mind flashed back to Sunday morning churchgoing when I was in the children's homes. It had been compulsory, part of the weekly routine. I hadn't been inside a church since those far-off days.

Emotion threatened to reduce me to tears. I slipped away from the others, making some excuse. They didn't notice me linger in the shadows and then fumble with the huge latch on the heavy church door. I slipped inside, closing it carefully behind me.

Inside, the silence was almost tangible. I stood and looked, breathing deeply the atmosphere of age, dust and duty. It felt good to be alone here. My eyes took in the ancient pews and stone pillars, the crimson blue and yellow of the stained-glass windows, the ivory candles. Near the back of the church was a faded blue velvet curtain. I pulled it back: just a little room with rows of coat hooks and some old chests of drawers. I pictured a choir of clean scrubbed little boys changing there into their white robes. But right now it was empty. The whole church was empty.

Suddenly I could hold back the tears no longer. I stumbled down the length of the aisle and fell down on the altar steps. I covered my head with my arms and sobbed like a baby – something that had been too hard to do for a very long time.

I cried for about two hours. I unloaded the emptiness of my life on to the altar steps, bleeding tears of bitterness over each disappointment. My search had taken me travelling along many different paths, but never to arrive at any safe or happy destination. Money – I'd had plenty of that in my time and it had left me impoverished. Drugs – they'd robbed me too, and given nothing in return that the dawn had not shown to be a fleeting dream. Parties. Girls. Crime. Flashy cars. Excitement and eroticism. I'd tasted it all and felt cheated. 'God! Jesus Christ! Whoever you are… please… I want love and peace and truth.'

All I'd ever seen of Christianity – the pious embargoes, the religious ceremonial and trappings – I didn't want any of that. It repulsed me. But if beyond it or behind it or within it there was one true God who was real and living and loving, then that night I knew that to know him was the only experience I would ever be satisfied with. To know that God. And to be loved by that God.

Finally, the tears stopped. I still felt heavy. But not so hopeless. It seemed a fresh beginning of sorts. Now I was tired. But I would come back here tomorrow. The air was clean. It seemed a place where there was enough stillness to let you get to God – if he was real.

It was about ten days later that I bumped into –

literally – two young guys in the street. One knew me at once, smiling broadly and reaching to shake my hand. As I stared back at his grinning face, close cropped hair and neat clothes, recognition came. It was Jeff, a boy I'd known from the drug scene of several years ago. But it wasn't the same Jeff.

'Yes, I used to be on drugs,' said Jeff. 'But not any more. I've come to know Jesus and he's changed my life completely. I don't need drugs any more.'

He and his friend Pete were keen to talk, but not all of it made sense to me. They told me where they were living and invited me round any time. And then they said they were going that evening to some kind of Christian meeting at Kingston Market Hall. It was free – would I go along?

'God willing,' I said to them, amused and intrigued at their eagerness to talk to me. Should I go? I wondered to myself. It didn't sound like my scene. But perhaps I should go along just to find out what it was all about.

It was after nine o'clock when I left the Apple Market Inn that night after a glass of wine alone and started to stroll home. I was quite surprised when I realised my route, unconsciously, was taking me right past the Market Hall. I found myself wrestling inside with the idea of going in, and finally I decided to creep in at the back.

To my astonishment the hall was packed with almost two hundred people. Someone was introduced and he got to his feet and began to address the audience with an urgency that was quite gripping. The content of what he was saying didn't register at all, but his transparency, the impression of honesty and sincerity, held me fascinated for quite some time.

When he sat down everyone started to sing, rather loudly, and then some of the audience – or was it a congregation? – started to wave their arms and some beat on tambourines. It was a clamour I couldn't stand, so I left as quietly as I had crept in. I went to Paul and Patsy's squat in Teddington and tried to talk to them about Jeff and Pete and what was going on in that hall. But they didn't want to talk and I gave up trying to get somewhere with them.

Why shouldn't I look into this Christianity? I asked myself. Shouldn't I give it the same chance as all the other religions or philosophies I'd pursued for the last six years? After all, there was nothing to lose.

The next evening I made my way to the house where Jeff and Pete were living. Jeff answered the door and took me through to the clean little kitchen. I explained that I wanted to find out more about Christianity. Jeff looked interested but wary, and I was afraid he would think I was trying to trick him. He didn't say much, except that if I was serious would I come back the next evening for a meal and a proper discussion?

'Well,' said Jeff, as I sat down the following evening with him, Pete and two of their friends called Dave and Kathy, 'When you come to Jesus Christ there is no one else to seek, no other god. You are satisfied. You will have no need or even desire for all those other things you've been involved in.'

They seemed to be talking my language. To find answers, to come to the end of a search – that was what I longed for. And here they were, telling me that this experience actually could be mine.

But what did it mean – to come to Christ?

We talked for a long time. Some things I grasped,

others made me frown with lack of understanding. Everybody, said Jeff, was a sinner, imperfect, not living up to God's standards. Well, I could accept that, even if I'd never used the word 'sin'. This sin, Jeff went on, made a barrier, or a huge gulf, between God and the people he had created and loved. Sin separated God from people. This, too, I not only understood but felt I had experienced. My own frustration at not being able to get through to God was real enough, and here was some explanation of the cause. But what could be done?

'That's where Jesus, God's Son, comes in.' said Dave.

Jesus, he said, was more than a prophet, more than a yogi or a mystic. He was God himself, come to earth in the form of a man to bring about reconciliation. By being killed innocently, crucified on a Roman cross, he paid the penalty God demanded for his people's sins. He paid the debt. But not just for the sin of those people living then, two thousand years ago. His death also wipes out the debt caused by people's sin ever since. He was raised from death, death had no power over him, and he's still alive.

This was hard. I wasn't sure I could believe this. That anyone should willingly die for others, though blameless himself, was the act of a martyr. It was something to admire. I admired it as a selfless act in history. But was there really more to it than this? Could the death of Jesus Christ, in that distant land, in that distant time, really be so powerful that right now in Kingston it could restore peace between the Almighty God and the wretched me?

I wasn't sure I could accept this, but the idea, the

possibility, excited me. If what they were saying was true, then this was actually the most dynamic thing I'd ever encountered!

The chill of the evening had settled into the room as we sat around our empty plates talking. I shivered and suddenly felt very tired, and desperate for a smoke. I knew I couldn't smoke in this clean and cared-for house. I said I ought to be going.

'Have you got a Bible?' one of them asked. I shook my head, and Dave reached for a small tattered book from a shelf, black with a zip around the edge.

'If you really want to understand about Jesus, about who he is and why he came to earth, then read the four Gospels – Matthew, Mark, Luke and John.' I slipped the Bible gratefully into my jacket pocket.

'Read them over and over, four times perhaps. And then come back and see us again.'

Over the next few weeks I spent many hours lying on my bed, alone in my room, reading and re-reading the Gospels. I wanted to understand it all, to know if what they had been telling me was true. I wanted to know about this thing they called sin. I could see, for example, that God would say adultery was sin. But according to this book it was sin even to look at a woman and think of adultery. What kind of standard was that?

Sometimes I closed the book and went to the pub. Other times, things I had done in past years, long forgotten or so I thought, would come into my mind with such vitality and force that I would cry and sob like a child. Events I hadn't recalled for years crowded into my head and felt like an unbearable weight over my eyes, crushing me.

Often as I crouched on my bed in misery I had a mental picture of myself lost in the deep folds and recesses of an immense black leather armchair. Ahead of me burned a bright white light. I kept glimpsing the light – even when it wasn't dazzling my eyes I knew it was always there. I was frightened of it. I knew I'd been living in darkness. Was Jesus the light? Was the Bible true? I turned away, burying my tear-stained face once more in those thick black comforting folds. I thought to myself, I believe Jesus is the light and all that the Gospels talk about is true. I knew I had to make the effort to tear myself away from all this darkness, and walk out into the light.

Paul and Patsy were puzzled by my behaviour during this period. And they made one or two attempts to 'bring me to my senses'. But the barrier between us was higher and wider all the time.

The newspapers at that time were full of stories about a teenage guru who was the head of something called the Divine Light Mission, coming to London. I was fascinated. Was he from God? I wanted to find out. I joined hundreds of people thronging to the big rallies being held to herald this new young genius leader.

'I've had my third eye opened. Have you?' The young girl sitting in the next seat stared at me, her mouth twisted with a weak smile. I started to make some kind of reply, but then there was a loud burst of clapping from the huge audience and I looked up to see the plump, smooth-skinned teenager take his place on a large throne in the centre of the stage.

The thirteen-year-old wonder spoke for almost two hours in broken expressionless English. I was astounded at the rapt attention of the crowd – for the words he spoke were simply strings of unrelated, illogical gibberish!

When the crowds began to disperse I went for a walk, finding myself heading away from the hall down the hill towards some trees. I was deep in my own thoughts when someone ran up behind me and slapped me on the back.

'Hey, it's Terry, isn't it!'

I recognised him as Timmy, a guy I'd met several times in Kingston and hadn't seen for ages. He'd moved to another flat and seemed keen to renew our friendship.

'Hold on,' I said, 'I'll take down your address.'

A friendly-looking couple of lads were sitting on the grass bank at the side of the path.

'Have you got a pen or pencil I can borrow? Just for a few seconds?' I asked them.

One pulled a short stub of a pencil from his back pocket. 'Why are you here this evening?' he asked me.

'The same reason as you, I guess,' I replied

I scribbled down Timmy's address on the back of a supermarket receipt. The two fellows who'd lent me the pencil were still chatting together at the side of the path. I handed it back.

'What do you mean – the same reason as us?' one asked.

'Well, I suppose you've just come from hearing the guru,' I ventured.

'Well, no! Actually, it's rather strange. You see, my friend here and I are both Christians. Earlier this evening we had a strong sense that we should come here tonight. I mean, we knew that God wanted us to come here – but we're not sure why!'

Nothing could have convinced me at that time that these Christians had not been 'sent' there that night for my benefit! I explained that I was searching to know God. But the guru tonight – he had got me all confused. Could they explain a few things?

They could and did! There was only one Messiah, Jesus, they told me as we sat on the grass under the trees. The young man all those people had been listening to was under evil influence and was a messenger of deceit, not truth.

Hearing all this, I felt really elated. I believed God had sent these two young men to protect me from going the wrong way. I listened and the clouds in my mind cleared. I went home and again took out my Bible with new enthusiasm to read and understand it. Each time I read it now, something else would come alive to me, the words seemed to leap off the page.

As I read day after day and incidents from the past continued to invade my mind, I was gradually aware of a feeling I couldn't at first identify. Bitterness was there. So were frustration and helplessness – they were old friends. Sorrow, yes, that too. But there was a shadow that stood alongside sorrow and I didn't know its name. Finally I could name it; it was remorse. Remorse made me look at my past life in a new light, from a different direction. I'd pleased myself, chosen for myself, lived for myself. For the first time a deep regret for so much of what I'd done welled up within me like an angry flood, threatening to drown me. It was almost more than I could bear.

As I read those pages in that well-thumbed little book, the words became more and more meaningful, more personal. It was an historical document, a piece of literature – but more than that now. I began to feel that it had a here-and-now relevance for the weak, burdened, desperate creature that was me. I began to see that not only was what I read true – but that it was true for me. Something was happening to me. I felt the need to be changed, to be clean – not only inside but outside, too. I began to take more care over the way I looked and dressed.

I stood on Jeff's doorstep again several weeks later.

'I've read it all, just like you said. And it's really making sense. I want to know Jesus. Can you show me how?'

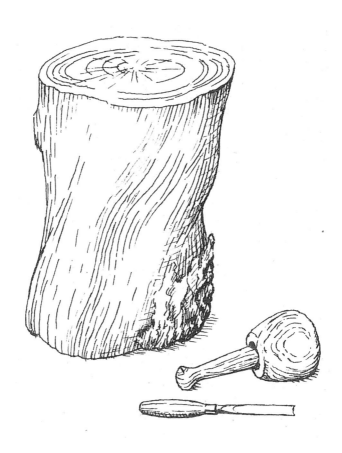

CHAPTER 8

I t seemed that I was just about to start life all over again. I still had questions, doubts and some confusion. But I couldn't deny the inner excitement that was urging me to find Jesus.

Dave thumbed through his Bible. 'There's a verse I want to show you here. What it says is that light and darkness can have no fellowship together, simply that.'

'What do you mean – light and darkness?'

'Someone who comes to Christ and is forgiven comes out of darkness into light. And light and darkness can't exist together. '

Becoming a Christian, they told me, was beginning a life of faith in God's Son, Jesus. Salvation was not dependent on what I was or had been but on the work of forgiveness by Jesus on the cross. This dawned on me with a tremendous feeling of release. I'd felt bound by the necessity to fulfill rituals of meditation, rules about not eating certain foods and so on. Christianity was not a programme or philosophy but a relationship with a loving friend who was all powerful.

We talked a lot more, and I grew more and more certain that I was arriving at the end of my long search. And I stood at the beginning of a new journey of discovery, the start of a totally new life. Yes, I would believe that Jesus had died that cruel death for me, wretched miserable specimen of humanity that I was.

Yes, I would put all the darkness of the past behind me and put my trust in Jesus for the future. I wanted to break with the past completely.

Dave prayed with me. When I stood to my feet, amazement swept over me! Impossible as it sounds, I felt as if a sack of coal had dropped from my back! I felt physically lighter, thinner almost! It was a sensation I could not remember ever having felt before in my life. My arms fell relaxed at my sides, my shoulders were not bowed, and I felt I could lift my head up in a new way!

A well of joy was bubbling up inside me with an energy that was overwhelming. I had the sense of being filled with words – but words I didn't understand, words I'd never heard before. It was some time later that I found out that this experience, of 'speaking in tongues' as it is called in the Bible, was a gift from God's Holy Spirit.

On my way home the sensation of wellbeing continued with me. I felt free, light, it was so good. Passing some open land I saw some daffodils and I couldn't resist picking them, loving their beauty, their yellowness, their greenness. I was elated. I made straight for Paul and Patsy's house in Teddington. I thrust the daffodils into Patsy's arms as she sat at the kitchen table. They both looked up at me, startled.

'Do you remember how a few weeks ago I said I was going to be with God? Well, it's true! I am, I mean, that is… I'm a Christian now. I'm different! Something's happened to me… tonight. It's changed me… it's Jesus… it's… !'

I couldn't explain it right then. Would I ever be able to? The certainty of the experience deep inside, taking root in me, was everything, was warm, was real.

Paul was engrossed in painting one of his little home-made drums, sprinkling it with signs of the Zodiac. He hardly looked up. Patsy seemed happy for me, but I could see she didn't understand.

'That's all right, Terry. We've all got to find our own way to travel,' she said, heavily. I turned away and left silently.

The next morning I awoke with the same sense of lightness, cleanness and freshness. And the next morning, and the next. But with it all came a growing awareness of the problems my new lifestyle was bringing with it. Everything I read in the Bible or heard from my new Christian friends contradicted the way I'd been living, even the way I'd been thinking up till this time. At the age of twenty-two all my carefully developed philosophy and values were being turned upside down. And it wasn't easy.

'Now look, Terry. This is going too far! They're expensive, man. If you don't want them anymore, then let's sell them. I know where we can get a decent price.'

I was burning all my books at the bottom of the garden. And Paul couldn't understand.

'You've flipped, man! You're out of your twisted mind!'

I added another thick volume on spiritualism to the flames, followed by several on transcendental meditation, then two or three Indian bamboo flutes. I relented and let Paul keep my big clay and pigskin drums, and kept just one little flute for myself.

'I know I've got to do it, Paul,' I argued.

'It says in the Bible, when Paul went round telling

people about Jesus, he found lots of evil things going on – people worshipping idols and practising magic. And it says that when they understood about Jesus, that's what they did – they burned their books. Selling them isn't enough. If they're bad for me they'd be bad for someone else.'

I watched the flames lick the blackening pages and felt a surge of relief. The more my life changed, God working in me, the more I saw that I needed to change. I'd given up drugs. Now I felt I wanted to give up cigarettes. But I couldn't.

I knew I should meet with other Christians regularly. But when I plucked up enough courage to go to church meetings I often felt rejected by the many cold stares I got there. One night I went along to a big Christian meeting at the Market Hall, and stood up and told everyone there I'd become a Christian. I fumbled my way through a few incoherent sentences and sat down, scarlet-faced. There were a few smiles of encouragement, but on the whole the atmosphere was stiff with embarrassment and even suspicion. Jeff, Dave and Pete helped me all they could. But some days I felt just like running away and hiding.

Maybe that was just what I needed to do – to run away and hide, to spend time sorting things out, licking my wounds and working out the new life I was living. I'd only been a Christian a few months and Jesus seemed increasingly close, a real friend. But I couldn't yet cope with the structure of organised church. Or with the straight ideas of so many of the people I was meeting. Maybe they couldn't cope with me. Anyway, I was beginning to feel as desperate as a caged animal. I wanted to change, but at the same time a lot of what I was being asked to do didn't make sense. And, even though they'd let me down, it hurt a little to be turning my back on Paul and Patsy. In spite of everything, their familiar world still held me tight in lots of ways. As to my new identity – it didn't yet fit properly, it wasn't comfortable.

Added to my confusion was a sense of being very vulnerable. All my defences were down, I was exposed. I was known all over this part of London. I was a man with a record – a housebreaker, thief, drug smuggler and rebel against society. My reputation was established here – with the police, local hippy communes, addicts, dealers. What chance had I against such odds? Would anyone believe that I'd changed? Would they allow me to? I wanted to confess to past mistakes, to wipe the slate clean and start again, maybe even make amends in some way for what I'd been. But would I get the chance to break out of the mould I'd made for myself?

Dave agreed with me when I said I needed to get away from London for a while. He knew of a place in Somerset, a community where some Christians lived, and he arranged for me to go there. I said goodbye to Paul and Patsy, packed my few belongings in a holdall and caught an overnight bus.

Arriving at the station in Somerset, I bought a packet of ten cigarettes, smoked one and threw the rest over a hedge. That was the last – I'd have to face up to going without now. Or could I? Finding it hard to go without a smoke, I retraced my steps and rescued the cigarettes from the litter behind the hedge, and then set off on the two-mile walk to the farmhouse. There a homely elderly woman, still in her dressing gown, her long hair in a huge thick plait down her back, wanted to cook me some breakfast. She made me wonderfully welcome.

I spent two weeks there, thinking things over, and received some spiritual help from Christians staying there. And I did finally kick my smoking habit, with help from the Lord. But I couldn't settle to stay any longer. And I had nowhere else to go but back to London.

In Kingston, a member of the fellowship to which Jeff and Pete belonged offered to put me up for a while. Andrew was an art teacher now – but some time before had experimented with drugs so he was able to relate to me in many ways.

I soon realised that my 'rest' in the country hadn't really been enough. Andrew was a great help – so much so that when he left on a week's teaching course I panicked, overwhelmed with a sense of my own inadequacy, which soon developed into the kind of acute paranoia I hadn't experienced since before I'd become a Christian. I convinced myself that if I went out, the streets would be peopled with faces from my past all staring and laughing at me. Ridiculous as I knew it to be in saner moments, for days I locked myself in the house, terrified to go outside. I felt that all the places associated with my past had terrific evil power over me. It was an experience God was to use to prove that he could solve any problem.

I couldn't live as a recluse for ever. For one thing, I needed to go shopping to buy some new shoes. The thought of walking through Kingston High Street was agonising. 'O God,' I cried, 'Help me!' And for two whole days I cried to God in desperation to take away my tears. The response to my desperate prayer came as a great relief. I saw plainly before me a vision of Christ holding a baby, cradling it in both arms. I knew that baby was me. And I knew then the overwhelming love that God had for me. My confidence in God my father soared to new heights.

On the bus and walking along the High Street, buying the shoes – I kept that vision constantly in my mind's eye, and somehow got through the ordeal. It might seem a trivial and even foolish incident to others. But that shopping expedition was a spiritual breakthrough for me. I'd experienced the reality of trusting God to take me through a problem. I felt I'd taken a major and positive step forward in proving that my faith was not a philosophy – it was power that worked!

Andrew returned from his course and life settled down for a few weeks. I continued to grapple with the challenge of my new lifestyle, often feeling low and defeated, at other times excited and elated. It was an up-and-down time. Being with ordinary 'straight' people was in itself a novel experience I had to learn to deal with. I had to reassess the everyday, look at everything with new eyes. And I struggled constantly to meet the high expectations of my newfound Christian friends.

Among my previous friends I'd occupied a position of some esteem – all based, I knew now, on vanity. How false it really had been I was only just beginning to see. Now, in the community of Christians in which I found myself, I had no role. And that in itself was very difficult to come to terms with. Many of the people at the fellowship seemed so very proper, living the kind of comfortable, clean, middle-class existence I'd previously despised and still felt to be very narrow. But the Bible said these were my brothers and sisters in Jesus Christ and I struggled to feel at ease with them.

I read about the Christian virtues in the Bible. Peace, joy, love, patience, humility… I had so much to learn. I was just like that baby in the vision, dependent on Jesus. I sighed as I prayed, stumbling over my own anguish. I needed to forget the things that were behind me, haunting me, and reach forward to grasp all that Jesus offered me. Humility was going to be one of the hardest things for me to learn, but I knew it was the way I had to go.

In the midst of all the hard lessons I was also learning that God had a sense of humour! It was during the time I was praying that I could understand humility that a Christian friend called Jennifer rang up to say she'd found a job for me – if I wanted it. What was it? I asked. Cleaning toilets! It was hard to accept and harder to do the job – but I knew it was God's way of answering my prayer about humility!

One night, as on so many other evenings, Andrew and I sat up late talking. He got so excited, so radiant, as he talked about his Christian experience that his whole face seemed to glow. It was as if his gingery hair was a halo of flames! Sharing together like this, it was as if the two parts of our conversation were like pieces of a jigsaw fitting effortlessly. Then he broke the news to me that he was moving out of London to a teaching post in Manchester.

Something in what he said made me determined that it was right for me to go with him. This, I was sure, was God's way of taking me out of my present depressed surroundings and giving me a fresh start. But, if I was to go with him, what about a job?

Four days before Andrew was due to leave for Manchester I was no closer to finding a way of going with him. Downhearted, I phoned the company and told them I couldn't carry on with the toilet cleaning job – I'd really had enough. Putting the phone down I sat staring into space, wondering what to do next. Then the phone rang. It was another department of the firm, obviously unaware that I had just rung in and said I was leaving. They were looking for someone prepared to take on a temporary cleaning job for several weeks up north and would I be interested? Where was it? I wanted to know. 'In Manchester,' replied the voice.

I was so excited I felt like doing a somersault. I agreed without hesitation, then rang the other department and apologised, asking them to forget my first phone call! This was so thrilling – to know that God really cared about me in every way. God was with me, right beside me, and speaking to me in a way I could understand.

Moving to Manchester was the first step in an entirely new part of my life. I'd been involved in many adventures before. Excitement and danger were not new to me. Now there was one huge difference. For the first time the adventure was happening within me – not without. The excitement was not in the visible happening, it was in the invisible changes and developments that were to happen inside the heart, mind and soul of the new, reborn me. Nothing could seem more inconsequential than living in a damp-smelling Manchester basement and going out to work to clean toilets. But now that I was learning to live each day with Jesus there was the stirring of new purpose and meaning in all that I did. And that change, slow and often difficult, revolutionised my life completely.

As it turned out, the job cleaning toilets didn't last long. My previous experiences made me excited and eager to know what God was going to give me to do next. I didn't have to wait long. I began to be offered small gardening jobs. This was something I did have a little experience in and enjoyed. One temporary gardening job was working for a Jewish man who owned a factory which made paper cups. This was a good few weeks. I often talked to the Jewish man about the difference Jesus was making in my life. Perhaps I was over-zealous in trying to convert him, too – his nickname for me became 'the prophet of doom'!

This period I spent working outside was a much-needed respite; it gave me time to think things over and absorb teaching from the Bible. The church I went along to in Manchester was quite tough going for me – the people there were pretty old-fashioned in their approach to things and I didn't feel at ease with them. But this did mean more time on my own to work things out for myself.

My next job was in a biscuit factory. This was more of a challenge. And there were times when I found it desperately hard. The routine of the eight-to-five day felt like a straitjacket inside which I squirmed, feeling bruised and battered. The monotony of standing in the middle of the huge bare tiled hall weighing out dollops of identical biscuit mix onto trays for the conveyor belt was more difficult than a prison sentence!

It was not just the work or the discipline of getting to and from the factory on time each day that made me feel old and tired. It was the terrific pressure of having to work alongside people who might just as well have been aliens from another planet. I'd always been very selective about the people I'd spent my time with, often so critical that I found myself with very few friends. I'd always been able to enjoy long periods of self-imposed isolation. But now there was no escape. I was surrounded by scores of factory workers with whom I had little or nothing in common. Not only that, but I was trying hard to come to terms with my changed personality. The swearing and filthy talk of the other workers caused me real distress. I was aware that before my conversion my own talk had been just as foul and blasphemous. I felt weak and nervous with them – and it showed. At lunch breaks it was hard even to sit with them: the sense of being different made me panic. And I could see that I made them uneasy, too. Before my conversion I would have had no time at all for people such as these, I'd have despised them. Now I knew it was Christ's teaching to love each one. Also, God's Word sustained me, where it says, 'And we know that all things work together for good to them that love God' (Romans 8:28, King James Bible).

However, times got hard for me. One day when it was particularly bad I threw off my white overalls and ran out of the main gate. Striding up the main road, who should I bump into but the pastor of the church I was attending! He had no sympathy whatever for me – and sent me straight back.

I remember one weekend when I was particularly low there was a speaker who came to the church who really encouraged me. Without knowing my situation at all, he spoke so helpfully about being a Christian in a factory setting, it gave me fresh heart. Knowing that God knew and cared about my situation was a great comfort.

Eventually, though, I moved on to another job, this time as a packer in a mail-order warehouse. This wasn't as tedious as the biscuit factory job and I found I could cope with the pressures much more easily. I began to find it easier to talk about my Christian experience with my workmates. I realised that where I worked was not as important to God as how I was spiritually growing at this time. God was exposing different areas of my life that he wanted dealt with and seeing this uplifted me.

After a time I was sometimes called on to deputise for the warehouse office manager when he was away or off sick. And it was on one of these days that a startling new idea came to me. Sitting at the boss's desk, an idea dropped into my head completely out of the blue. I should be my own boss. Work for myself – with a window cleaning round.

It was such a surprising idea, not at all like me, that I sat bolt upright in the chair.

'Eh?' I said, addressing the pile of order forms in front of me. 'Is this your idea, God? It doesn't seem like one of mine. If it is you, then you must open the way for me to do it.'

A little amused, I put it out of my head and turned my attention to the paperwork. At lunchtime I went home for something to eat and Keith, a Christian friend who lived in the flat with me, came in. He was grinning broadly and rubbing his hands together. It was a characteristic pose. Keith was always full of bounce and optimism, and it did me good just to be with him.

'Terry, you'll never guess,' he said, pushing his long blond hair from his eyes.

'Praise the Lord! Hallelujah! I met up with an old friend this morning – and he's offered me a window cleaning round in Marple!'

I was amazed! Totally amazed! I explained to Keith what had been going through my head just hours before. So much excitement was welling up inside me I didn't know how to express it.

'I believe that this really is something from God!' I said.

'OK,' he said, slowly. 'I can believe that all right. Do you think we should work together? Partners on this round?'

I nodded.

'But we don't want to plunge into it just like that. I feel really confident – but I'm going to ask God to give us some kind of sign that this really is what he wants. Let's be certain.'

For the rest of that day, though, I felt buoyed up by a growing cushion of confidence. This must be right. I met Keith after work and we went to get some fish and chips for tea. Queuing at the counter, we took our places behind two ladies deep in conversation together.

'. . . And d'you know, Mrs Smith, it's practically eight months since I laid eyes on the wretched man. Call 'imself a window cleaner! A'course my Tom would do it 'isself, if it wasn't fer 'is back. I said to our Audrey, would you believe it, I said, place the size o' Marple and there's only one window cleaner to be 'ad – and 'ee doesn't bother to turn up. Disgustin' I calls it!'

Keith and I looked at each other. This had to be something a bit more than coincidence. 'Excuse me,' I said, 'were you talking about a window cleaning round in Marple?'

'What does the Bible say about faith?' I said to Keith, as we tucked into our fish and chips back at the flat.

'It's the assurance of things hoped for and the conviction of things not seen – what about that!' (Hebrews 11:1, New American Standard Bible).

Well, we took over that second round without paying a penny for it, and it was right next to the one Keith had been offered. Usually the going rate for a round like the one the Lord had given us was about £200. Praise God!

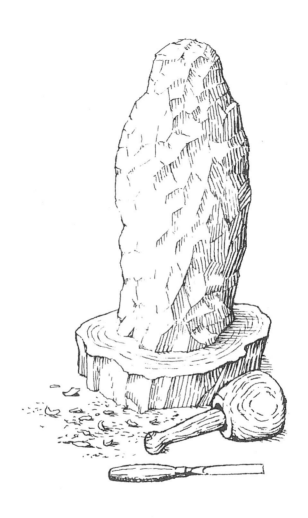

CHAPTER 9

I was not physically strong. Many years of abusing my body with drugs plus the several illnesses I had suffered had taken their toll. So I found the window cleaning job tough and physically very demanding. But God had given it to me – so it meant more than just a job of work.

In the winter there was no respite from the icy cold winds as I clung to my ladder washing windows with numb hands. Keith, so it turned out, was not even as hardy as I was, and after a while sheer exhaustion persuaded him to hand the whole round over to me. I carried on, though at times sorely tempted myself to chuck it all in. Often, my face reddened and sore with the biting weather, my hands stinging and chapped, I was on the verge of cursing God for ever leading me this way. But how many times when I was at the absolute end of my endurance would the front door of the house open, and a young housewife or a dear old lady would pop her head out and offer me a steaming cup of tea or coffee!

'Just thought you might like a cuppa.'

'Thank you. That's very kind,' I would choke, climbing down gratefully. And inside, 'Thank you, Jesus,' I would be saying.

Working on my own I felt more able to deal with the pressures of leading a socially acceptable life. There were no time clocks. No difficult people threatening my attempts at leading a 'straight' life. No deadlines except my own. No pressures but the need to wash enough windows to pay the rent and food bill and keep my regular customers happy.

And because the job was not mentally demanding, even though it was often physically very tough, it was a good time to be growing spiritually. I had time to look up a verse or two in my Bible as I worked and I could think about what they meant as I wrestled with the wash leather and bucket. I felt I was grasping lots of things about what was in the Bible that until now had remained shrouded or indistinct. I was beginning to understand the power of the Scriptures, and the energy of the Holy Spirit seemed to be opening my inner eyes to all kinds of things. I found I was not struggling so much to try to understand what it all meant with my own limited understanding – instead it was as if the Holy Spirit was teaching me. When I had first become a Christian I had periods of great doubts when I would question myself over and over again about the validity of what had happened to me. Who was talking to me and guiding me? Was it really God's Holy Spirit? Or was it the Devil? Then I read in John's Gospel, 'But the Comforter, which is the Holy Ghost, whom the Father will send in my name, he shall teach you all things.' So that gave me great peace. I began to stop struggling and listen more. What I couldn't understand I would leave to the Holy Spirit until it was time for him to teach me about it. And I learned, too, to live in today, not to be filled with anxiety and worry about tomorrow.

I began to think more and more often of going back to Kingston. I got news from home that an old hippy

132

friend I'd known on the drug scene had got converted to Christianity and that made me feel really excited about the possibility of going back there. It was almost three years now since I'd walked those streets and seen those familiar places and faces. I was different. I began to feel that not only could I cope with the old temptations but that I had grown sufficiently to be able to trust the Lord for my own needs and to reach out towards others in need. Would I be able to tell others of my experience of Christ? I thought of my old friends with a longing to share with them something of the new life I was beginning to enjoy, the new purpose I was increasingly aware of. I thought about the detention centre where I'd spent so much time in my teenage years and felt desperate to be able to talk to the young people there about the different kind of future that Jesus could give them. I thought, too, about the kind of loneliness I'd endured in prison and wanted to help those still suffering it. But, keen as I was to go back to Kingston, I was determined to wait for God's timing. I was aware that to go back before I was ready would be a big mistake. So I prayed and waited.

While all these thoughts were in my mind, Keith and I went to stay with one of his friends who lived near Yeovil. Lennie had been a colonel's batman or butler and lived in a caravan in a remote part of the Somerset countryside. He was a laughing, smiling person who was often singing – usually songs praising God! He was easily excited and it was not at all unusual to see him take his hankie from his top pocket and wave it in the air as he swayed or danced from side to side in church!

It was on our visit to Lennie that we heard about Stan, who lived on a beautiful farm about ten miles away from Lennie's caravan. He was a Christian and his home was always, it seemed, 'open house' to his brothers and sisters in Christ. Lennie took us to meet him. Stan was the kind of rare person who is overflowing with love for others, who only has to see you to reach out and put his arm round you. I loved him at once, and his wonderful welcoming home. It was like stepping into another world for me. I marvelled over it all as he took me around, patiently pointing out and explaining everything out to me. There were lots of animals... pigs, chickens, cats sleeping in the sun on the haystacks, a blind Labrador curled up on the doorstep. He showed us his 'praise place' – a lovely spot on the top of a hill overlooking the farmhouse, surrounded by huge rhododendron bushes. Everything about the place was so wholesome, right down to the hot bread that Stan took from the big old kitchen ovens.

Leaving the farm, Keith and I hadn't got far when our car broke down and refused to be started by any means. 'Never mind,' I said, trying not to sound as unhappy as I felt. '"All things work together for good to those that love God" – that's what it says in the Bible.' (Romans 8:28, King James Bible)

We hitched a lift the few miles back to Stan's farm, and he was more than happy for us to stay the night and promised to help us rescue our car the next morning. That evening we sat in a little whitewashed room watching the glow of the embers from the log fire dying down in the stillness of the night. We talked together about Jesus and then began to pray for one another. Keith and I prayed for Stan's foot, which was causing him some pain due to an ingrowing toenail and he looked up with tears on his face to say that he was feeling immediate release from the pain. It was the most wonderful night; it seemed as if it must last forever. The car breaking down had 'worked for good'! It seemed like the closest thing I had ever known to heaven. To be in complete harmony of mind and spirit with others who loved the same Lord – it was an experience I learned to love that weekend and have delighted in finding along the way ever since. Oh, to stay in a place like this! To be close to nature seemed to mean to be closer to God. Was I really thinking of returning to the grimy gutters and grey roofs of Kingston?

On Monday morning I took the glow of that Somerset farm weekend back with me as I got on with cleaning windows. But the following weekend was to prove an equally important one. The Sunday morning sermon at church was based on Elijah from the Old Testament in the Bible. In it God told Elijah to go from his place of hiding by the brook of Cherith to Zarephath – a town which means the 'place of refining'.

There are times when it seems as if a preacher is speaking just to you and this was one of those times. I felt that God was telling me to leave Manchester and return to my 'place of refining'. It was time now for me to return to face the test of being on home ground. And there I would be refined; I was ready to lose some of my rough edges and to be made into what God wanted me to be. So now I was sure that this really was to be the next step, I began to pray and wait to see how the Lord would make the way open for it to work out.

Tentatively, I made a couple of visits back home for a day or two, visiting the Kingston Fellowship and talking to the Christians there about it, asking them to pray too about all the practical implications of a move back home such as a place to live and a job. I was persuaded in my own mind that I would be returning, that it would work out.

While everything was still in this state of indecision, something quite unexpected and totally wonderful happened to me. I fell in love.

It was July of 1975 and I was going with some friends to a Christian conference holiday week at Blaythwaite in the Lake District. It was a great holiday, attended by hundreds of young Christian people from all over the country. The night before we were all due to go home, everyone stayed on drinking coffee in the big marquee after the meeting was over. I found myself standing close to a slim, attractive girl with dark brown hair, whom I had noticed earlier in the week several times. Tonight I couldn't take my eyes off her.

Nothing like this had ever happened to me. I felt ridiculous and awkward as I tried to pluck up courage to go and talk to her. There was a thunderstorm outside competing with the music and sound of excited voices. I went outside and shut myself in the toilet so I could think. Dare I go and introduce myself to her? I went back inside. She was still there. She had beautiful dark brown eyes. I went back out into the toilet and shut myself in the toilet again, trying to calm my feelings. What would I say to her? What did men say to attractive girls? It was a long time since I'd thought about it. But this wasn't just any pretty girl at any ordinary event. This was a Christian girl and I was a Christian guy, and we were at a Christian event. Even more confusing. I didn't know how to handle it at all.

After several visits to the toilet to pray – I was really anxious to know what God thought about me approaching her! – I did manage to go and to speak to her. Sue was a nursery nurse and had come on holiday with a group of friends from a large fellowship in Bradford. Yes, she would come for a walk outside with me. But, no, she wouldn't hold my hand!

So that was the start of our love. The fifty miles between my home and hers made meeting difficult, but within a few months we were both certain that we loved each other in that deep and lasting way that reached out to the commitment of marriage. After the disastrous relationships of my younger days I'd never thought I would get married. But somehow I'd known almost as soon as I'd set my eyes on her that Sue was for me. And Sue confessed that a Christian friend had told her that she was to meet the man who would become her husband on that week's holiday. She was such a caring, thoughtful person I loved her more and more each time we met.

We began to talk about plans for the future. How would I be able to support her? Sue showed me the part of the Bible which tells the parable of the talents. She said God would expect me to use my talents (Matthew 25:14-30, King James Bible) – my gifts or abilities. I didn't understand, and then she pointed to the medieval chess set I'd been carving out of clay. Since childhood, carving had been a fascination for me, but I'd never imagined it could provide me with a job.

Now I continued to make plans for moving to Kingston – but taking a wife with me. Eight months after our first meeting we got engaged and set a date for the wedding three months ahead. I went to Kingston in advance when some friends from the Kingston Fellowship, Paul and Jean, offered to put me up for a while. Within a few short weeks I had a job in a car radiator repair shop – and a home. The house we eventually got had been rented to Jean's father and mother, and belonged to a missionary couple working in Morocco. It fell vacant and it was agreed that Sue and I could rent it. Taking God at his word – it says in the Bible (Philippians 4:19) that 'my God shall supply all your need according to his riches in glory by Christ Jesus' – we began to pray for furniture and within days I heard of a whole flat full of furniture that was unwanted, from which I was able to salvage a bed, wardrobe and lots of other useful items including some tools. Cupboards and equipment for the kitchen were offered to us from another source.

Incredibly, when we moved into the little house in Teddington, God had indeed supplied all our needs. Hardly the kind of dream home most newly-weds sigh for. No, this was better. We had God, each other and love. And the wonderful assurance and security of being in God's will. It was perfect.

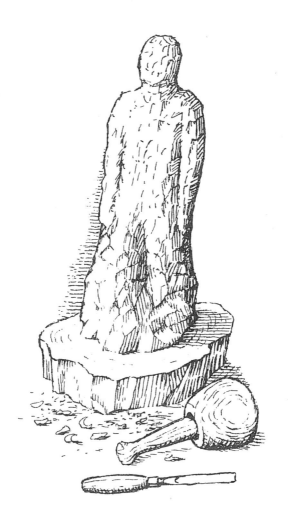

CHAPTER 10

I'd come a long way – with the Lord's help. I was learning to follow Christ and the change that made in my life was a constant source of wonder to me. I had the kind of ordinary joys of life I'd thought I'd never know – a home, friends, and a lovely and loving wife who encouraged me in everything I tried to do. I could look back at the dishevelled hippy wandering the back streets of Morocco, sick, half-starved and without hope, and I hardly recognised him any more. Praise God for that!

The first six months at the car radiator workshop were great! I tried hard to get on with the other men there, about a dozen of them. They all seemed open to listen to the Gospel, particularly one man called Kevin. He was a man in his fifties who worked on the bench opposite me.

One afternoon it was Kevin who threw me down a challenge I couldn't refuse.

'You're always on about God this and God that. If he's so clever, what about my arthritis then? Could he do somethin' about that?'

'Sure, Kevin. If you're serious. God really can heal you.'

Kevin looked at his arm. Some days the pain was so bad he would bang his arm against the wall repeatedly.

'Well, what do I have to do, then?'

I sat him down at his bench and laid my hand on the arm, then began to pray out loud. I was so scared of looking a fool I hardly knew what I was saying.

A few minutes passed and I became aware that Kevin was moving his arm.

'Hey, it's gone! It's gone!' He was swinging his arm wildly in every direction.

I was thrilled and excited and of course in the days that followed talked more and more to Kevin about my conversion and the power of prayer. And, foolishly, I confided in Kevin much of the darkness of my past life. I told him too much. And somehow in a few short weeks he changed from being someone who was open to the Gospel to someone who became an enemy. He began to take every opportunity to refer to my past and ridicule my faith so maliciously that I began to believe it was an attack by the devil himself.

To go into the details of what became Kevin's campaign of persecution against me would profit little. I was forced to endure the extremes of evil gossip, blasphemy and false accusations. And the constant plague of 'practical jokes' ranged from having doors slammed in my face to being threatened with a hammer and finding urine in my tea mug, even an attempt to gas me.

Incredibly, I managed to live with all this for three years – but not without terrific cost. Getting up to go to work each day was torment. Sue sometimes pleaded with me to leave the job. She was desperately unhappy about what I had to put up with.

'I can't leave, Sue,' I would say, kissing her goodbye. 'Don't you see? I prayed for a job – God gave me this one. I can't leave until I'm sure it's what he wants. I've asked him, but he's silent. I must stay until he says go.'

Hadn't the Lord told me in Manchester that this would be a Zarephath, a 'place of refining'? Because he was with me it would be a worthwhile experience, although painful. I knew I needed to see Christ as the light and victory in the situation, not run away from it.

During this time my thinking was many times reinforced by verses from the Bible that talked about the power of God that is available to believers. One verse in particular from which I drew great strength was from Philippians 3, in the Amplified Bible: 'For my determined purpose is that I may know Him – that I may progressively become more deeply and intimately acquainted with Him, perceiving and recognising and understanding the wonders of His Person more strongly and more clearly. And that I may in that same way come to know the power outflowing from His resurrection which it exerts over believers.'

The terrific power that was actually strong enough to raise Jesus from the dead – that tremendous force was potentially mine because I belonged to him! It was a revelation that bowled me over; it was too much to take in! I needed to exercise that power, to use it, to let it work through me. The ambition to be filled with that resurrection power stayed at the front of my thoughts for months during that dark period.

However, there was a battle going on. The inner and outer conflict of each day was having a suffocating effect on me. I felt heavy, pressed down, and began to have recurrent pains in my head. Sometimes as I left work I felt so ill and tense I would get off the bus with a few miles to walk through the park and woodlands, so that I could pray and relax a little before seeing Sue.

In spite of all the difficulties, I took comfort in my relationship with God that was still deepening and growing. Bible verses were a tremendous help to me and I continued the habit I had started on the window cleaning round, of making notes in a little book to encourage myself, sometimes a verse that was especially appropriate, sometimes a reminder of the way in which God had answered prayer.

And even though some days were so depressing, this was a time when I had great assurance in my prayers and several people were healed by God when I prayed for them. On one occasion Sue and I were asked to put up a couple of young Christian girls from Devon. One of them had a very bad allergy. Her eyes watered, her nose ran and she was having difficulty breathing. As we sat at lunch together the thought of the tremendous power of God was uppermost in my mind. I asked if I could pray for her for healing. Lots of ministers had prayed for her, without success, she said.

After lunch I laid my hands on her head and prayed for her, and afterwards told her to believe that she was healed. I didn't look at her; I didn't want to look for the evidence but to have faith that she was healed. It was later as we got into the car to go out that I turned to her.

'You are healed, aren't you,' I said.

'Yes,' she replied, 'praise God, all the symptoms are completely gone!'

One day, after a hard day at the workshop, feeling

too low to go home straight away, I called in to see my younger brother Philip who was working in a menswear shop not far away. Working with him temporarily on the staff was a young white South African called Patrick and I got talking with him. He told me that he had been seeking God in a monastery in Oxford but had left. I felt drawn to him at once. His mind and heart seemed so open and sincere. He jotted down his address for me on a scrap of paper and I promised to call and see him some time.

For the next two weeks, every time I prayed or read my Bible I had an overwhelming sense of God telling me to go and visit him. But I'd lost his address! The scrap of paper just wasn't to be found anywhere. I went to see Philip again. Patrick had left the shop – and, no, Philip had no idea where he lived.

Under great conviction one evening I set off for Surbiton, where I thought I remembered Patrick had his bedsit. I wandered the streets, praying that God would guide me to the right house. It still amazes me how simply it all happened – I just went up to a door, knocked on it, and Patrick himself answered!

He was surprised but pleased to see me, and asked me in.

'It's amazing that you should just turn up – tonight of all nights!' he said.

Amazing? He didn't know just how amazing it was! I was still feeling stunned by the way God had led me to the house.

'I've just come back from the pub, where someone was arguing about religion. There's a few questions I've got on my mind. Perhaps you could clear them up for me?'

'Tell me,' I invited. 'I know God's sent me here tonight.'

Patrick talked. For weeks, he said, he'd been having a rather strange experience. Every time he closed his eyes he could see the image of Christ on a cross and he couldn't stop thinking about it.

'Tonight that cross is more real than ever. What does it mean? Somehow even the atmosphere feels different tonight, as if God is all around me. Ninety per cent of me wants God – but the other ten per cent... ' His voice trailed away and he sat tensely on the edge of his armchair, staring at the carpet.

'The other ten per cent needs to know that the way to God is not through the religious life you were trying to lead at that monastery – but through trusting in Jesus Christ,' I said.

I began to tell him about Jesus on the cross, and how by giving up his life in that horrific death he offers forgiveness of sins to us. Suddenly Patrick began to understand how it was possible to have a personal relationship with God through belief in Jesus. We prayed together, Patrick asking for forgiveness of sins and me asking for God to give him a new life, I reached out and laid my hands lightly on his shoulders – and as I did so he was literally flung backwards in his chair with his arms high by a force that wasn't from either of us.

He laughed, and shouted, 'Hallelujah! I've seen this on the TV but I never thought it could happen to me!' He had his arms stretched up in the air, thanking and praising God.

I threw my Bible on the chair for him and stood up. 'I must go,' I said. 'My wife will be wondering what's happened to me. But read this and ask God to reveal himself to you tonight and I'll come round again tomorrow.'

I saw him the next day. He said he had decided to go out to help his parents in Mozambique. It had been on his mind for a while. They ran a farm there and he'd had a letter to say the Communists were threatening to take it over. I begged him not to go so soon – but he wouldn't listen to me. I never saw or heard of him again. But I was grateful to God for allowing me this experience to help me understand what his resurrection power could mean in the day-to-day life of an ordinary person like me. And I'm grateful to God for showing me the importance of obeying his prompting to go and see Patrick. If I hadn't, he may never have had the opportunity of salvation again. Praise God!

Soon after this experience God had something else to teach me – through a little canary.

One day; arriving at the yard for work earlier than the rest of the men, I glimpsed a patch of bright yellow amid the drab grey machinery.

A little pet canary was sitting on a pipe near one of the acid tanks. It must have escaped from a cage and it had been through a tough time. It had been raining most of the night and its feathers were so sodden it couldn't fly. It looked a pitiful sight.

On the spur of the moment I climbed up towards it. My outstretched hand was just inches from the bird when it panicked and flew off, very unsteadily.

A small incident – but it made me think a lot. I should have thrown a net or a coat over it. I might have hurt it by bringing it to the ground like that, maybe even broken its wing. But even so I would have saved its life, I would have rescued it and could have nursed it back to health. By forcing it to fly off bedraggled and exhausted in broad daylight I'd almost certainly sentenced it to death by one means or another.

It was an interesting thought – that by hurting it in the first place I might have saved its life in the long term. It began to dawn on me that this might be exactly what God was doing in my life. Why was God putting me through this bad work experience? Was he hurting me to save me? Was there some purpose to it all? As I passed through these difficult situations, the Lord was showing me more and more that he wanted me to know how these things were working for my good.

This gave me more strength and confidence in the Lord. Over the next few weeks I wrote and copied out a little booklet called 'Changed', which told what God had done for me and for others in dying on the cross. I handed it round to the men in the yard and to people I met outside work.

Reading of the great adventures of God's people in the Bible, my own struggles at work seemed pathetic. 'The people that do know their God shall be strong and do exploits' I read in Daniel 11:32. God's people were heroes. What about me? There was another verse that constantly came to my mind, too, where it says that God has prepared 'works' for us to do. 'For we are His workmanship, created in Christ Jesus for good works, which God prepared beforehand, that we should walk in them' (Ephesians 2:10, NASB). How was I fulfilling that in any way?

How good God was to me! He gave me an answer! Because it was during this time that something did happen to make me a hero – albeit a reluctant hero.

Sue and I were on our way one day to visit my sister Suzanne. My mind was full of the great gulf that lay between my own struggles and the 'exploits' of the real men of God.

I'd been praying that God would show me these 'works'. And as we left home that morning I felt warm in the awareness of the presence of God with me. I felt God was so close to me that something exciting was surely going to happen. Not a premonition... but the thrill of expectancy that I was learning to associate with being in touch with God.

It was a Saturday, and there were crowds of shoppers thronging Kingston Bridge as we went to cross. But, wait a minute! I've told this story before! This is where my book opens – the day when I jumped, or rather tripped, from the bridge parapet to rescue a depressed young man who'd thrown himself over in the expectation of ending his miserable life.

So, inadequate as I was, God proved to me that day that when I was willing to be used by him then he could perform 'exploits' through me. The saving of Vic's life was great. But there was part of the experience that was in a way more wonderful to me. It was the thrill of knowing that God had brought this about and had prepared me for it. Vic later repented of his past life and was converted to Christ.

These incidents kept me going when the daily routine was difficult, when the persecution at work was at its keenest. There were other bright times, too, not least of which was the arrival of our firstborn son Nathan.

But, after three long years at the radiator repair yard and in spite of these encouragements, I then entered a period of really black depression caused by the unrelenting persecution that confused me and made me unsure of God's will. Feeling beaten, defeated, I decided I could take it no more. I handed in my notice.

I got a job immediately on a milk round. I was in such a demoralised state I wasn't sure if I would be able to cope with the responsibility of it. The accounting side of the work proved very difficult. Over the first few weeks I lost about £100 – mainly due to my own errors, some through cheating by customers that I was too naive to cope with. I did get all the money back but then, as I started to get the paperwork under some kind of control, some rather unusual circumstances began to crop up. People began to complain about non-delivery of their daily pintas, when I knew perfectly well I had delivered them. So strange did it become that I actually started to wonder if this was the Lord's way of taking me out of the job. I didn't have to wonder long. Four or five customers cancelled their orders and the dairy dismissed me.

After eight months of getting up at 4am to go on the round and often working well into the evening on the figure work, it was a terrific shock to find myself out of work. I felt suddenly that my life had come to a total standstill. The pressure of the recent years weighed on me and I felt crushed by the burden of my own inadequacy.

For two whole days I lay face down on a sun bed outside in the yard in a state of semi-consciousness. I couldn't think. I had no mind. No will. Nothing. Nothing but fear and a gnawing emptiness.

I was living a nightmare. I was falling to bits. I couldn't even talk to Sue. No one could help me. Only

God. I made up my mind to pray and pray until I got through to him again. I prayed. Fell asleep. Awoke and prayed again. Slept some more. Prayed again. I felt as if all Hell was let loose on me.

Near the end of the second day I was feeling desperate to fill the emptiness in my heart with something from God. I reached for the Bible lying on the ground by the bed. I opened it and read: 'It is God who is all the while effectually at work in you – energising and creating in you the power and desire – both to will and to work for his good pleasure and satisfaction and delight' (Philippians 2:13, Amplified Bible).

That was it! That was really it! God was clearly speaking to me through this verse, telling me that he was working in me, making me willing... making me willing even when I didn't feel willing... giving me the power and desire to do his will.

The thought began to put me together. For the first time I felt free to think about what I really wanted to do and confident that my will and God's will could be one and the same. And the instant I turned my mind to consider what desire there was in my heart about what I should do with my life I was surprised to find that there were things tucked away there unrecognised.

I pieced together the thoughts. My desire was this – to live entirely by faith and trust in God, to preach his message and to rely on him to meet the needs of myself and my family.

But, even as this revelation came, I knew that I wasn't yet ready for that life. So did I have a practical desire for the present? Yes. I was startled to discover that deep down I did have a very real desire. I wanted to be a craftsman!

CHAPTER 11

Why? Where had that strong desire come from? I saw a picture in my mind of a small resentful boy standing all alone facing a wall. It was me, in that children's home so long ago, hurting, being punished. And for what? For whittling away at a lump of chalk with a toy drill. As long as I could remember, I'd always loved whittling sticks or lumps of clay or chalk. It came naturally. I enjoyed it. I might even be good at it. Could I be a woodcarver? I remembered what Sue had said to me years before when she'd watched me working away at a set of chess pieces in Manchester. Then I had been experimenting with mounds of clay baked in the oven, scraping away for hours to achieve some level of satisfaction.

'You've got a talent for it. Use it for God,' Sue had said.

This was enough to put me back on my feet. I wasn't sure where to begin, but I was convinced God was showing me that I should work with my hands. I'd already done a lot of experimenting in my spare time, using different rubber solutions to make moulds to reproduce chess pieces in resin, I got to work again, getting books on carving and practising endlessly on odd pieces of wood. Recognisable shapes began to emerge. Animals mostly, or birds.

I prayed for a shed to work in – and almost immediately a friend told me about her mother's next-door neighbour who wanted a shed taken away. I prayed for tools – and was given the opportunity to buy practically everything I needed to equip the shed for a fraction of the real price.

Being creative in this way, actually producing something of value with my own hands, was the start of a new confidence and a healing closeness with God. I spent hours in my little shed in the garden – and worked for God and with God. As I shaped and caressed my rough sawn block and began to see emerging the antlers of a stag or the wing of a bird, I could almost feel God at work in my life, shaping and loving me. It wasn't all plain sailing, but then, didn't I sometimes have to take the roughest of files to my wood in my search for the best result?

Working when you have to is boring, but when it's a heart's desire because it's God's will, then it's perfect! Working in the will of the Lord is a delight! And he gives us the power to accomplish it.

I knew it wasn't going to be easy at first to make any money from my work, slow as it was. I decided to look for a job until my work improved enough to guarantee regular work. At the local employment exchange I saw an advertisement for a driver with a joinery business. Bad memories of my time with the men at the radiator repair yard came flooding back and I turned away. But when I returned three weeks later I had the nagging feeling that God wanted me to take that job; sure enough, it was still on the board and I applied.

As it turned out, my fears were unfounded. It was a pleasant small family company of high-class joiners. And, as well as feeding us for the next year or so, the job had one other very valuable benefit – the carpenters, who got to know of my woodcarving, often passed me generous offcuts of really good quality wood which kept me well supplied in my shed for a long time.

I tried my hand at lots of different ideas, from miniature regimental soldiers to tall relief sculptures and statues that soon lined the hall.

But the real breakthrough, which enabled me to set up on my own completely, came when I was given a £2,000 contract for some intricate carving for a stately home in the Guildford area. The story of how that happened is a real miracle in itself.

Sue and I decided that it would be a good idea to get some leaflets printed to advertise my woodcarving services. I was beginning to get one or two orders for small items such as carved house signs. We were put in touch with a Christian designer who worked from home and he said he'd help us produce a brochure. Talking it over with him, he mentioned he knew of an old woodcarver working in Kingston for a church furnishing company. I decided I'd go and see him, but when I arrived at the dilapidated workshops I was told that the old woodcarver had left.

'Are you a woodcarver?' one of the men asked.

When I said, 'Yes!' nodding enthusiastically, he reached for some plans for some carving designs.

'Could you do something like this?' he asked.

I looked at the intricate carved architraves very carefully. What did God want from me? The detail in the work was on a level I'd never before attempted. Just thinking about it put my mind in a whirl.

'Yes,' I answered, with as much confidence as I could manage. 'Yes, I could do something like that.' I felt certain that it was God's will for me to take on this work.

The work took me five months to complete – a period I measured out not only in time but in tears. But as I saw the lovely shapes emerging after hours of patient work, I began to see that it was a testimony to the goodness of God in all that he had done in my life. I began to feel that at long last what God wanted for me was coming into the light. I was discovering the real me because of the love of God and the healing power that it brought to me.

Confirmation that God wanted me to work at home like this came when I got planning permission to have a work shed in my back garden which seemed unlikely to be granted. A neighbour who had applied was refused.

Carving new shapes from old... that was at long last happening in my life, too. And at long last I felt I could cope with helping others. During this time I began to make contacts with prisons and remand homes and started to visit there, hesitantly at first but with growing confidence when I saw that the men and boys I talked to were interested in finding out what had happened to someone who really knew by experience what they were going through. Since my time in Manchester I'd longed to visit prisoners; as soon as I'd moved back to Kingston I had asked to visit the local detention centre, but a new padre had just started there and we didn't really get on too well, so it hadn't worked out. Three years later I met a chaplain who invited me to speak at Feltham Borstal and that's how I was finally able to start visiting the prisons. Also, our church fellowship had a singing group which used to visit prisons and I began to use this as an opportunity to speak about my experience of coming to God. Following that, I was given invitations to speak at many prisons, including Wormwood Scrubs, Wandsworth, and Winchester. On one occasion eight prisoners at Pentonville were converted after I shared my story with them.

One afternoon I was in Twickenham Library, in the reference section. I often went there to study books to get ideas for designs for my woodworking. I looked up as a creaking of the door announced the arrival of someone else. An elderly, gentle-looking man with an umbrella hanging from his wrist and a big smile on his face searched the room with his eyes, obviously looking for someone. When he saw me he marched right over and thrust a piece of folded paper into my hand.

'God wants me to give you this,' he said, still smiling broadly. Then he turned briskly and disappeared round the shelves of books.

I was astounded. I'd never seen the man before and never had anything like this happen to me. I unfolded the bit of paper and read a Bible reference. I could hardly wait to get home and look it up. The verse was from Matthew 7:7. 'Keep on asking and it will be given you; keep on seeking and you will find; keep on knocking (reverently) and the door will be opened to you' (Amplified Bible).

It was an exciting way for God to confirm to me that I was going in the right direction. I would keep on seeking, keep on with God, keep on wanting to do his will. Having found his will, I wasn't going to let it go easily, no matter how tough the going got.

One day I was out delivering some carved house numbers to a garden centre. It was five o'clock on a cold February evening and as I pulled out of the centre in my old Austin car I turned left to make for home, for Sue, my little boy Nathan and newly-arrived baby Gareth.

Changing up into fourth gear, I was startled suddenly to see blazing headlights coming towards me – on my side of the road! I jammed on my brakes, but knew as I did so that a crash was inevitable. I caught one glimpse of the other driver's terrified white face as his car ploughed into mine at almost sixty miles an hour. I felt my body pressed hard on to the steering wheel, but at the same time I felt a great well of peace surge up within me. I got out of the car. The other driver was in a state of shock and I sensed that I had to be careful what I said, otherwise he was likely to punch me in the face! He was a big fellow and his eyes were full of anger.

We studied the extensive damage done to both cars, and then I became aware of the traffic hold-up we were causing. I helped the other driver push his car onto the grass verge, and backed mine up into the garden centre driveway. Standing next to the large display greenhouse, we exchanged addresses, and some of the staff at the centre who were just closing down the business for the night came over and helped me remove my mangled bumper from the front wheel and check the rest of the car to see if it was safe for me to drive.

By this time I was becoming aware that the entire left side of my body was feeling bruised and ached badly. But the worst of it was my hand. I was almost certain that two of my fingers were broken. I was concerned about the immediate difficulty of driving home – yet strangely enough the problem of how I was going to carve with an injured hand did not bother me. I felt certain this was another situation God was going to use to teach me something important, believing that the deeper the situation, the greater the revelation that would come from God to meet my need.

I managed to drive in some pain to the home of our friends Paul and Jean, where Sue and the children had been spending that afternoon. Paul drove me to the local hospital for some X-rays, which confirmed that two of my fingers were broken.

Sue was shocked and upset, but I found myself telling her that God would use this situation for our good, and not to be anxious about it.

The next morning I sat in my shed and tried to come to terms with the fact that I simply couldn't work with my injured hand. What was God saying through this experience? I prayed and listened hard. I felt an overwhelming sense of God being with me, all around me, in the shed. And it seemed to me that he was saying that we'd trusted him to bring jobs in, but that we'd been trusting in my ability to get through the work to bring us in money each week. Now, God was saying, he was going to teach us to trust him, literally, for our daily bread. Hadn't I said that my heart's desire was to live by faith in God?

This experience was vital in the development of our walk with God, as it really extended our trust, confidence in and dependence on him in a deeper way. It was sometimes hard not to feel anxious as the days passed and I was unable to work and therefore could count on no income at all from my carving. Then when my fingers slowly began to heal there didn't seem to be any jobs coming in!

However, God's Word gave us great assurance and joy as a family. For three weeks we lived by what we had in the larder and the garden. Finally, we knew we were reduced to our very last meal. Sue cooked some broccoli leaves with some herbs and a few other bits and pieces and that was all we had.

We both knew God wouldn't press us any further. Now that we had nothing at all we waited to see how God would meet our needs. We were hungry, but there was also a strange sense of excitement with us. We had no evidence, but had faith that God would be true to his word in supplying all our needs. God doesn't lie.

There was a knock at the front door and we both jumped up. It was Ken and Doreen, a Christian couple we knew, just passing and calling in to see how we were. We chatted with them for a while and then they got up to go. Carrying Gareth in my arms, I saw them out through the front door. As he left, Ken pushed something into my back pocket. Putting Gareth down, I reached in – and pulled out a £20 note!

'Hey, what makes you think I need this, Ken?' I said.

'Oh, I got a little word from the Lord.'

'Well, if it's from the Lord – that's all right, then,' I said, grinning.

'Well, Terry, you know me… I wouldn't give you a penny if it was my own way,' he replied, laughing.

No, it wasn't his way. It was God's way, all right! And how wonderful it was! That money was more precious to us than any I'd ever earned But even more precious was the assurance of God's love for us. The next day a Christian neighbour came in and asked me to carve a house sign for her. She wanted a wooden plaque bearing the words 'Jehovah Jireh', meaning 'God will provide'. You can imagine the joy I had working on that carving. Hallelujah! God was keeping his word to us. Praise him!

Life was certainly exciting now that God was in charge. Often we could hardly believe the amazing answers to prayer that he gave us – not just for ourselves, but for others with whom we came in contact.

Like Laura, for instance. Laura lived just a few doors away, and we had heard that she'd had a breakdown. One morning as we were praying, Sue and I were conscious of the Lord telling us to be more specific in our prayers, not to ask for vague generalities.

'Sue, I keep feeling... I can't describe it... a sort of burning feeling deep down and I see the name "Laura". I think we should pray for that lady.'

Afterwards I asked Sue if she would go and visit Laura.

'But, what shall I say?'

'I don't know, but I think you should go. She hasn't been seen in the street for weeks and she may be feeling frightened and scared of leaving the house and lonely, too.'

'I'll go – but keep praying for me.'

Laura's mother-in-law answered the door to Sue, which made her feel even more nervous. Sue asked to see Laura and was shown into the lounge. Laura was sitting there looking pale and tired. Sue did her best to talk in a friendly way for nearly half an hour, but there was little sign of any warm reaction from Laura. Finally, she stood up.

'Well, I must get back to Terry and the boys,' she

said, awkwardly.

Half turning to the door, Sue added hesitantly, 'Laura, we are praying for you. And Jesus Christ really does care about you.'

Those were the words it seemed that Laura's numbed mind had been waiting to hear.

'Don't go! Please stay and talk. I've been in such darkness, been so depressed. You know, I've even thought of asking Terry to pray for me, I know you go to church.'

Laura poured out her heart to Sue and Sue returned home to me in a much more confident way than she had left. We felt humble and grateful that Laura had been open to hear about Jesus, and also that the Holy Spirit was reaching us to pray for specific real needs.

A week later, Laura called in to see us. She looked very wobbly and told us she had been to the doctor to get some more pills. She was still feeling very depressed and felt like giving up on life. There was a brief conversation about the children but Laura left before we were really able to talk to her much about herself and the Lord. Some days later, though, Sue called me in from the shed to find Laura again in our little back room. This time she really did want to talk business.

'I really need help. I'm sleeping very badly. Every time I close my eyes I see a long dark tunnel. Ahead is light and freshness. What does it all mean?'

'Well, we're glad you came round,' I said. 'That's exactly the kind of picture I used to have a lot before I became a Christian.'

'Really? Do you remember any more about it?' she asked.

'Not really. Some years ago when I came to know Jesus Christ I saw that I needed to put it all behind me and so that's exactly what I did. When you meet Jesus you're out of the dark and into that light and freshness, the past is gone and you can live for today.'

We talked for a long time and then she left – to think it over, she said. We didn't see her for another two weeks – but when she did we could see immediately that she'd had a dramatic change in her life. Her face and eyes were so clear and her voice was full of life and energy. She was happy.

'One night last week I felt more confused and depressed than ever,' she said. 'I got really upset with the children and locked myself in the bathroom. I just wanted to get away, to be on my own. I kept seeing that long dark tunnel I told you about, and I remember crying out, "Am I always going to be like this? How can I get along that tunnel and out the end?"

'I was feeling pretty desperate. Then I saw Jesus! He was in the tunnel with me and he was holding a lamp. The top part of him was shining. I just knew it was Jesus. I started to cry and cry. I must have cried for some time. But then I saw myself gliding... gliding down that tunnel with Jesus. And out the other end!

'I went into the bedroom and began to get ready for bed. Jack came in and said something about me looking different – radiant, he said I was. So I told him all about it. He says I'm lucky to have had an experience like it. I don't really know what it all means, but it's like you were saying the other day. I feel Jesus has saved me from my sins and from my past – and I'm never going back there again.'

Some time later, Laura gave her testimony in the

church next door, and was baptised. Weeks later, as someone was preaching, she received the baptism of the Holy Spirit and began to speak in other tongues. Praise God!

We had quite a different result when we began to pray for someone else in our street, a woman in her late sixties who was a wheelchair user. We used to meet her husband in the street and ask him how she was. He was a sulky man, full of self-pity, and we wondered how she coped with both her own illness and him. The more we prayed for her, the more we felt we should speak to her about Jesus. But how?

One evening, after two weeks of feeling under growing conviction from God, I decided I could put if off no longer. Dressing in some decent clothes after finishing work in the shed, I went along to their home and knocked on the door, holding my Bible behind my back.

'Could I see your wife?' I asked tentatively.

The man who had opened the door to me stared, suspicion written all over his furrowed brow.

'What for?' he mumbled.

'Well, I've just got some really good news I wanted to tell her about.'

Just then a door opened and the woman came into the hall, slowly feeling her way along the wall.

'You haven't come to change my religion, I hope,' she said, softly.

'I just wanted to have a chat,' I replied.

I could see they were both rather wary, but they let me in and led me through to their small back room where a colour TV was on at top volume. The woman and I sat either side of a drop leaf dining-table, while her husband settled himself in an armchair in the corner of the room – one eye on me and the other on the blaring television set.

I said I'd been praying for her and told her something of my own experience of finding God to be real. She had been brought up a Catholic, she said, and told me a bit about herself. She seemed really interested in what I had to say. She began to tell me how she thought some people could be good and upright without Christianity. And I told her about Nicodemus, a man in the Bible who seemed to be a really good man, a religious leader, and yet Jesus told him that, just like everyone else, he needed to be 'born again'.

I reached for my Bible from where I'd slipped it inside my coat. And as I did so there was a loud outburst from the man.

'That's it! That's enough,' he said.

So saying, he hitched his trousers up and stamped out, presumably to the outside toilet.

'You've been lucky to have this much time. Usually he won't let anyone in to see me, not even the priest,' said the woman, whispering behind her hand.

The man returned, grim-faced, and then without a word showed me out of the house.

It was ten days later before I saw him again, walking down the road. Seeing me, he furtively darted down a side turning. When I got home I mentioned it to Sue.

'Oh, Terry, I heard this morning. His wife's died, I'm afraid.'

I had explained to her about forgiveness of sins and the Christian life. Had she responded to that before she died? Or had she slipped from one Hell into another? I shuddered. But I was so glad I had obeyed

God in going to speak to her. How would I have lived with myself if I had not?

It was not long after all our convictions about specific prayer that we went through a time of several months when we really rushed our prayer time, and it was again through a time of financial hardship that God brought us back to trusting and seeking him.

One evening we realised that we were totally out of money. The next day we needed to pay our milk bill, which was about £6. We were ashamed to admit that we had been lacking in prayer and prayed for forgiveness and a fresh start, asking God to give us £20 for our immediate needs.

The next morning we went downstairs, fully expecting to find a cheque or some cash had come in the post – but the doormat was empty. Had God let us down? Surely not. We could hear the milk float and the chink of bottles coming up the street, and looking out of the window could see the milkman only three or four doors away – and usually he didn't come until after lunch.

We got down on our knees and prayed hard. Even without the postman, God had other ways of providing, even at the last moment, I told Sue.

'With God all things are possible' I quoted from Matthew 19:26. 'It could even come out of thin air. It could even come through the letter box right now,' I said.

Even as we knelt there, and before the words were out of my mouth, a cascade of six letters fell through the letter box. The postman had been late. We opened them hurriedly – and one contained £30! We had barely got up off our knees when the milkman knocked at the door to collect his money!

'Seek ye first the Kingdom of God and His righteousness and all these things shall be added unto you.' How often did we quote that verse from Matthew to each other and yet how often did we have to learn the vital truth that was summed up in it.

That year, about a fortnight before Christmas, Sue made out a shopping list of groceries.

'We shall need about £25 – and that doesn't include the meat,' she said, looking at me.

'God does say "take no thought for the morrow, what you shall eat or what you shall drink",' I reminded her.

Still, the words sounded a bit hollow and unreal. Christmas only comes once a year. Surely God would want us to have enough. We'd got used to buying our food often a day at a time as the money came in. But with shops closing over Christmas, surely it would be reasonable to shop for the holiday period in advance? I felt concerned about it.

But it was Sue who cheered me up. The next morning she tore up the shopping list in front of me.

'You're right,' she said. 'The first thing my eyes fell on in my Bible this morning was those verses from Matthew. Of course God can provide our Christmas shopping needs.' She told me she had a really strong feeling that our food would be provided.

Two days later a woman came to the door to deliver a huge traditional Christmas hamper. It was an unwanted prize in a competition. It had been won by a relative who wasn't a Christian – but had decided to give it away to us!

'Sue,' I said, 'I am fully persuaded that God will

provide all our needs, whether we ourselves are in want or in abundance.'

'Do you know, Terry,' said Sue, as she looked at the lovely hamper, 'there's no fresh meat here – but I believe God is going to give that to us, too!'

The next day a friend we hadn't seen for months arrived with a gift of two frozen chickens and some mincemeat. How good God was to us!

Time after time, in recent years and right up to today, God has been faithful in providing for us at times when the resources were exhausted, both materially and spiritually. We are continually grateful to the Lord for the way he leads us and keeps us.

It's so wonderful getting to know the Lord in such a personal way. God is certainly not confined to a church building. One day, as I was having a bath, God spoke to me, saying, 'I want you to write a book that it will bring glory and strength to my name'. I knew it was God saying this, but I didn't know exactly what it meant then. My prayer is that all who read this will see God in it.

'Brothers, think of what you were when you were called. Not many of you were wise by human standards; not many were influential; nor many were of noble birth. But God chose the foolish things of the world to shame the wise; God chose the weak things of the world to shame the strong. He chose the lowly things of this world and the despised things – and the things that are not – to nullify the things that are, so that no one may boast before him.' (I Corinthians 1:26-29, NIV)

This account tells, as well as I know how, the story of what became my search. I reached the end of that search when God brought me to Christ and. I want to let others on life's road who are still searching know that there is purpose, meaning and fulfilment in a life surrendered to God.

Although my search is over, I believe the adventures that began the day when I came to Jesus will never end.